SEMINGTON PAST AND PRESENT

Front cover: Semington Bridge and Canal;
Back cover: Interior of St. George's Church, Semington

SEMINGTON
~ *Past and Present* ~

Edited by Gabrielle & Douglas Firmager

With the following members of
SEMINGTON HISTORY PROJECT
without whose active participation this
book would not have been produced:

Mr Dave Barnett
Mr & Mrs M. Bennett
Mr & Mrs G. Butcher
Mrs June Fry
Mrs Muriel Gover
Mr Philip Humphries
Mrs Sylvie Lloyd
Mr Victor May
Mrs Pam Mortimer
Mrs Victoria Shackleton

together with assistance from many others,
whose names will be found on the following pages

WITH FUNDING FROM THE MILLENNIUM COMMISSION

Published in 2002 by
ELSP in association with
Semington History Project Group

ELSP
1 The Shambles
Bradford on Avon
Wiltshire BA15 1JS

For editorial enquiries please contact
SEMINGTON HISTORY PROJECT GROUP
72[B] High Street
Semington
Wiltshire BA14 6JR

Design and typesetting by
Ex Libris Press
Bradford on Avon

Printed by Cromwell Press
Trowbridge

ISBN 1 903341 83 3

CONTENTS

	Other Contributors	6
	Acknowledgements	7
	Abbreviations	8
	Introduction	9
1	THE EVOLUTION OF SEMINGTON	11
2	THE CHURCHES	25
3	POPULATION, OCCUPATIONS & HOUSING	43
4	MAPS & ARCHAEOLOGY	57
5	EDUCATION	71
6	PUBLIC HOUSES, COACHING, TOLL ROADS	87
7	LISTED BUILDINGS	95
8	FARMING, FLORA & FAUNA, THE HUNT	111
9	THE MILLS, BRICKYARD, ABATTOIR, TANNERY, BOAT BUILDING	127
10	CANALS & RAILWAY	137
11	REMINISCENCES	151
12	MELKSHAM UNION WORKHOUSE	175
13	COMMUNITY GROUPS AND THE VILLAGE HALL	185
14	THE FUTURE	198
	Bibliography	200
	Index	203

OTHER CONTRIBUTORS

Mrs Betty Bonham
Mrs Glenys Bright
Major Michael Bruges
Mrs Iris Bryant
Mrs G Burbidge
Mr Eric Clifford
Mrs Angela Crossley
Mr & Mrs Earley
Mrs Suzanne Gilbert
Mrs Jeannette Greer
Mr & Mrs Ferneyhough
Mr Kevin Lockwood
The Late Dr. McBryde at Church Farm
The Masters Family at Manor Farm
Mrs Betty Noad
Mrs Maureen Norton
Mr Robert Oglesby
Mrs E. Robinson
Sally Scott-White
Mrs Betty Smith
Mr and Mrs Stainer at Outmarsh Farm
Mr and Mrs Stiles
Mr Gerald Taylor
Mr L. Taylor
Mrs Julia Wade
Mr and Mrs Waracker
Sally Wills
Mr and Mrs Woodward

ACKNOWLEDGEMENTS

Our thanks are due to the following people and/or organisations who have offered advice or their services in the course of this investigation:

To Community First and Voluntary Action, Swindon, and the Millennium Commission for funding this project from the proceeds of the National Lottery. Also to Bob Bradshaw, Alison Crawford and Rosemary Hopgood for all their help and advice.

To Michael Marshman (the County Local Studies Librarian) for an informative talk to the Semington History Group and for continuous guidance and assistance; also to Daphne Perkins and other members of staff of the Wiltshire Reference Library whose unfailing cheerfulness when faced with persistent requests for obscure volumes made working in the Library a pleasure.

To Steven Hobbs (County Archivist) and the staff of the County Record Office, whose deep personal knowledge of the contents of the archives never ceased to amaze us. Also Roy Canham, the County Archaeologist, for so generously providing us with photographs, and Mrs P. Slocombe, of the Wiltshire Buildings Record, for providing information on listed buildings in Semington. Coupled with this must go our thanks to all individuals and organisations who have cared enough to deposit their papers in the archives so that others may benefit from the fantastic store of information that is available..

To Brett Dolman, Curator of topographical and antiquarian collections, the British Library, for confirming the existence of a document relating to Semington.

To Rod Priddle, David Hyde and John Sawtell, for generous permission to reproduce their pictures previously published in *The Holt to Devizes Line*.

To the Editor of the *Wiltshire Times*, for giving permission for extracts from articles and photographs to be reproduced in this book.

To Sally Scott-White and *The Wiltshire Wildlife Trust* for producing information on local flora and fauna.

.To Sylvie Lloyd, for providing the drawings for the chapter on “Flora and Fauna”.

To Victoria Shackleton, for her research into St George’s School Records.

To Desmond Clarke for the Holt railway pictures

To all the property owners whose premises are pictured in this volume

To Julia Wade, Pete Vooght, Emma Jackson and Stuart Taylor for their help with the article on Queen Elizabeth II's Golden Jubilee celebrations

To Ashton Farms (Turnpike Foods Ltd.) for their donation towards the publication costs

To Hazel and Vic Gott for coming to our assistance whenever we had problems with the computer

To David Daniels for performing the valuable but onerous task of proof-reading.

To Roger Jones of Ex Libris Press for his forbearance and understanding during the preparation of this book

Whilst the editors have made every attempt to trace and credit all persons who have provided pictures for this work there are a few unsourced entries. We apologise to anyone whose photographs may come under this category and hope that they will be pleased to see their efforts preserved in print for posterity. Despite every effort being made to ensure correctness any errors are solely the fault of the editors.

Uncredited photographs, "Steam" Swindon, and those on the front and back covers are by Douglas Firmager

The illustrations on pages 89, 91 and 134 are from *Stagecoach and Mail in the Days of Yore*

ABBREVIATIONS

WRO	Wiltshire & Swindon Record Office
VCH	Victoria County History
WHS	Wiltshire History Society
WANHS	Wiltshire Archaeological & Natural History Society
WN&Q	Wiltshire Notes & Queries
K & A	Kennet & Avon Canal
W & B	Wilts & Berks Canal

INTRODUCTION

Unlike Steeple Steeple Ashton and nearby Whaddon, the village of Semington does not appear in the Domesday Book (for reasons which may appear later in the course of this book). Nor is it mentioned in subsequent commentaries by such travellers as Leland[1] (in his *Itinerary,* written during the 1540s when Henry VIII reigned) or Daniel Defoe[2] (in *A Tour Through the Whole Island of Great Britain* in 1724-27) or William Cobbett[3] (whose *Rural Rides* appeared in 1830).

However, early in 1913 the poet, Edward Thomas, was commissioned by his publishers, Thomas Nelson & Sons, to take a bicycle ride from London to the Quantocks and to write a book about it. Thomas left London before Easter 1913 and cycled via Guildford and Dunbridge over Salisbury Plain to Trowbridge and Shepton Mallet, thence to Bridgwater and the sea. In Chapter VI, headed *The Avon, The Biss, The Frome,* he leaves Trowbridge and records:

> "As far as Hilperton and the "Lion and Fiddle", houses and fields alternated along the road, but after that I entered a broad elmy country of young corn and new-ploughed land sweeping gradually away on my right up to grass slopes, and to the foot of dark Roundway Down and pale Beacon Hill, above Devizes. Far to the left the meadow land swelled up into the wooded high land above Lacock, Corsham, and Bath. Under elms near Semington the threshing-machine boomed; its unchanging note mingled with a hiss at the addition of each sheaf. Otherwise the earth was the rooks', heaven was the larks', and I rode easily on along the good level road somewhere between the two."[4]

The book, entitled *The Pursuit of Spring,* was published in April 1914. When War was declared in August 1914 Edward Thomas enlisted in the Army. He was killed at Arras in April 1917, at the age of 39.

When Thomas cycled through Semington on his way to Melksham, Holt and Staverton, the village would have appeared much as it had for several generations. The 1837 Tithe Map shows a long street leading from the "Ragged Smock" (now the roundabout) towards Melksham, containing a number of houses, some large, some small, each with its garden or orchard. Apart from one largish house at the beginning of Pound Lane, only Church Street contained any further housing, plus the Church itself, Church Farm and Manor Farm. South of the "Ragged Smock" Littlemarsh looked as self-contained as it does today. The entire village was, of course, surrounded by farmland.

Sadly the elms, once so much a feature of the area around Semington, fell victim to the dreaded Dutch Elm disease in the 1970s.

It was not until after the Second World War that any real changes came about, with the decline of farming and the advent of so much more housing. One of the main objects of this book is to try to show present and future generations what it would have been like to live in Semington in years gone by.

Semington is a typical example of an older village, wherein the present population of "newcomers" outnumbers the genuine local inhabitants in the year 2002 by about ten to one. It is to those who were born in Semington and to those who have lived here for some fifty years or more to whom thanks are owed, because without their reminiscences and the photographs generously given from treasured family collections this book would not have been possible.

References

1 Chandler, John (ed.), *John Leland's Itinerary* (circa 1546). Stroud, Alan Sutton: 1993

2 Defoe, Daniel, *A Tour Through the Whole Island of Great Britain,* 1724-27. Harmondsworth, Penguin: Reprinted 1979.

3 Cobbett, William, *Rural Rides*, 1830, Harmondsworth, Penguin: Reprinted 1964.

4 Thomas, Edward, *The Pursuit of Spring*, London, Thos. Nelson & Sons: 1914.

Chapter 1

THE EVOLUTION OF SEMINGTON

HISTORICAL LANDMARKS

NATIONAL	DATE	LOCAL
	100 AD	
ROMAN OCCUPATION		
	400 AD	
DARK AGES		
	550	
ANGLO-SAXONS		
	900	
	973	EDGAR CROWNED KING IN BATH Bequeaths Ashton Manor to Romsey Abbey
WILLIAM THE CONQUEROR	1066	
DOMESDAY BOOK	1080-90	3 Mills recorded in Steeple Ashton
	1087	
	1100	
		St Mary's Church, Whaddon, built
	1200	
	1252	Steeple Ashton Church built
	1281	Dedication to St Mary the Virgin of Steeple Ashton Church recorded
	1300	St George's Chapel probably built by now
	1400	
	1470	Residents of Semington ask for chaplain to officiate at services

	1500	Littleton Wood Farmhouse built, Nos 26 & 27 Church St. Semington built, Church Farmhouse built, Littleton Mill Farmhouse built, Littleton Green Farmhouse built.
	1600	Manor Farm, Semington, built
ENGLISH CIVIL WAR	1642-46	
	1643	Battle of Roundway Down
EXECUTION OF KING CHARLES I	1649	
	1698	"Manor House" in High Street built
	1700	Outmarsh Farmhouse built
	1790s	Semington House built, Old Coach House built, Aqueduct and K & A Canal built
	1800	
	1801	Riot at Littleton Mill, which burnt down
	1802	Wilts & Berks Canal Lockhouse built
	1803	Execution of Thomas Helliker
	1810	K & A Canal Lockhouse built
POOR LAW ACT	1834	
CORONATION OF QUEEN VICTORIA	1837	
	1838	Melksham Union Workhouse built
	1859	Semington School built
GOLDEN JUBILEE OF QUEEN VICTORIA	1887	
	1894	Semington Parish Council inaugurated
	1906	Semington Railway Halt opened
CORONATION OF KING GEORGE V	1910	
WORLD WAR I	1914-18	
	1933	Semington Village Hall built
	1934	First street lights in Semington
KING GEORGE V JUBILEE	1935	
	1936	Twice yearly refuse collection instituted
KING GEORGE VI CORONATION	1937	

	1938	Airplane from RAF Yatesbury crashes in Church field

Tiger Moth Aircraft in ploughed field, 1938. (Courtesy Wiltshire Times*)*

	1939	30 mile limit proposed by Parish Council
WORLD WAR II	1939-45	
	1942	Semington adopts HMS *Avon Vale*
CORONATION OF QUEEN ELIZABETH II	1953	
	1966	Semington Halt closed 30 mph Order published
	1967	Tenders invited for new school
	1968	By-pass scheme put forward by Parish Council
GOLDEN JUBILEE OF QUEEN ELIZABETH II	2002	Bypass works commence

Kennet & Avon Canal side-cut.

The buildings referred to in this chapter are dealt with under the heading of "Listed Buildings" in Chapter 7.

The burning down of Littleton Mill and the subsequent hanging of Thomas Helliker can be found detailed in Chapter 9: "The Mills, etc."

For further information on Semington Station please see Chapter 10: "Canals and Railway".

Melksham Union Workhouse (later known as St George's Hospital) has a fascinating history covered in Chapter 12.

* * *

Semington lies in the Hundred of Whorwellsdown (a Hundred being a sub-division of a county and having its own court). As mentioned elsewhere, the Abbess of Romsey was the Lady of this Hundred and exercised large powers over the population as well as over the property. One authority[1] suggests that the name Whorwellsdown comes from *Har-welles-dun*, implying that the Lord (or in this case, Lady) of the Hundred held her court by a hoar, or ancient well-on-a-down.

However, according to *The Place Names of Wiltshire*[2] there were a number of different forms which referred to the Hundred: *wereforesdone* in 964, *Weruedesdona* in 1086, *Wervedeston* in 1279, also *Wherflesdone*, and in 1565 *Whorlesdown*. This authority states that the first element in the name is in Old English *hwyrfel*, which is used elsewhere to describe a well-marked circular hill, hence *hwirfles-dun*, later Whorwellsdown. It is suggested that Whorwellsdown must be identified with the low rounded hill on which the boundaries of Steeple Ashton, Edington, Bratton and West Ashton meet, near Cresswell Down Farm.

Steeple Ashton has a Charter, which concludes:

> "If anyone shall venture rashly to infringe this my grant and refuse to make satisfaction, let him be dragged down with heavy chains round his neck among the fire-breathing regions of black devils"

The boundaries of Ashton follow: "From Semington round by Keevil and Edyndon to the River Biss then by Merebrook and Southwick (in North Bradley) across to Trowbridge, Hilperton Moor and back to Semington"[3]

The name Semington has undergone a number of changes over the centuries. In 1249 it was *Semelton*, also *Semeleton*, *Sempneton* in 1258,

Semelynton in 1300, *Sempleton* in 1327, *Sembletone* in a Wiltshire Tax List of 1332,[4] *Semington* in 1470, *Semyngton* in 1545 and 1576[5] and *Simenton* in 1675. The first part of the name contains the old name of the stream, in 964 as *Semnet*, therefore tun on the Semnet; and Semington Brook is *aqua de Semelton* in the Somerset Assize Rolls of 1249.[6]

The first indication of any people living in Semington, according to the *Victoria County History of Wiltshire*, (Vol.VIII) is when in the 12th century the Abbess of Romsey conferred lands to "Richard, son of Michael, son of Herlewin, which included 1/2 hide in Semington, held freely and 1/2 hide there held by 10s. a year" (a "hide" being a measure of as much land which a team of 8 oxen could plough in a year – between 60 and 120 acres, according to the quality of the land). In the mid 13th century some of these lands were held by Peter Fitzmichael of Semington, and then by his widow, Alice. The lands then seem to have been acquired, probably through marriage, by the Tinhead family. What happened after that is not clear, but by the middle of the 15th century these particular lands were held by Robert Long, who already had another estate in Semington (together with the Mill at Littleton mentioned above). The two properties together were first called the MANOR of SEMINGTON in 1522 and descended in the Long family to Sir Robert Long, who succeeded his father, Sir Harry Long, in 1556. Some time before 1591 the freehold was sold to the Brouncker family, Lords of the Manor of Melksham. The estate was sold again, and again – widows remarried and their husbands acquired an interest which went to their sons, or their sons' wives – until it descended, still as the Manor of Semington, to George Pitt, who left it to his grandson, George, Baron Rivers, who held it in 1780. By 1800 it had been sold to the Duke of Somerset, by which time the buildings known as Church Farm and Manor Farm had been in existence since at least the 16th century.[7]

SEMINGTON AND THE CIVIL WAR

Very few written records survive regarding Semington's involvement with the Civil War, yet one of the most famous episodes - the defeat of the Parliamentary forces at Roundway Down on 13th July 1643 – must have had some repercussions, for surely the sight and sound of the battle would have been seen and heard in the village.

By October 1644 Chalfield Manor had been occupied by Parliament and a garrison established there which was financed by taxing the local towns and villages. The accounts kept by William Tarrant the "Receiver" or "Collector" for the garrison have survived for the years 1645-46 and give the following information:

"The Hundred of Whorlesdowne

From	Semington	£5. 0. 0
	Steeple Ashton	16. 6. 6
	West Ashton	18. 19. 0
	Bradley and Southweeke	39. 19. 0
		£80. 4. 6

Note: In the left hand margin is written, in the same hand and ink, the note: This hundred is in the enemy's quarters"[8]

Roundway Down

The fact that Semington is mentioned once only in this two-year period as having paid tax to Chalfield, and does not appear to have provided any farm or other produce at that time, whereas vast quantities of goods of all kind, and services in the form of manual work, were received from the inhabitants of Trowbridge, Bradford on Avon, Broughton Gifford and Holt, gives the impression that Semington was either too near the Royalist garrison at Devizes or that the inhabitants had enough sympathy with the other side to avoid anything more than an occasional cash payment to the Parliamentary forces.

Some evidence for the latter theory comes from the notes made by Wiltshire Buildings Record on a house, now known as 26 and 27 Church Street, Semington, and believed to have been the Manor House of Semington at that time:

"In July 1646, the Parliamentary Committee for Wiltshire records that 'John Kitson of Semington in this Countie, gent., being a Soldier in Arms (for the King) at Oxford, upon the surrender thereof, hath appeared before this Committee, desiring a Certificate of the valuation of his Copiehould and lands in Semington aforesaid.... He is seized in fee to him and his heires of & in one Messuage and diverse lands and tenements ... in Semington, of the yerely value before these troubles of £30.00.00. His mother Ann Kitson enioyes the third part of theis lands during her life for her dower..."

These notes go on to record that John Kitson subsequently sold his property in Semington to John Twyford, yeoman, for £600, and was fined £45 on 3rd December 1646 by the Parliamentary Committee.[9]

WHADDON

Although geographically near, there is no direct road from Semington to Whaddon. It lies not in Whorwellsdown but in Melsham Hundred, so it seems somewhat illogical that it should have been merged with Semington in 1894. It would appear either to have been a question of "balance" on the part of the Boundary Commissioners or of a distinct desire by the local residents to disassociate themselves from Hilperton, (and therefore Trowbridge). Nevertheless the only way to get to Whaddon by road is via Hilperton, although there is a footpath from Semington.

It is an ancient parish and quite isolated: the Manor was held by Alvric of Melksham, and was assessed at 3 hides in the Domesday Book. In 1242 it was held by Henry de Whaddon and remained in his family until 1342, when it was acquired by Thomas Gore. From then on the estate passed through a nunber of hands, including those of Thomas, Lord Seymour of Sudeley. Soon after his execution in 1549 the main part of the Manor, including a fulling mill, was bought by Henry Long (in 1555) and remained for many years in the Long family. One of Henry Long's sons, Edward, founded the line of the family later known as of Rood Ashton. A Manor House, reputed to have been built in the 16th century once stood on the site of Whaddon Grove Farm. It was destroyed by fire in 1835.

The church is known locally as ST MARY THE VIRGIN, although in 1886 the Ordnance Survey gave the name as St Michael. It was built at least as early as the 12th century and altered in the 14th century. In 1879, at the

Whaddon Church

instigation of W. P. Long, the present chancel was built, the porch reconstructed, a bell-cote for two bells rebuilt at the west end and the whole church re-roofed and covered with stone slates. There is a mausoleum of the Long family and other monuments, including gravestones in the floor, to various members of the Long family.[10]

RECOLLECTIONS OF THE CELEBRATIONS FOR QUEEN VICTORIA'S JUBILEE, 1887, WRITTEN IN 1889 BY MR HENRY STOCKWELL

SEMINGTON, 27 MAY 1889. Date of writing the following recollections of the Jubilee of the accession to the Throne of Queen Victoria of Great Britain and Ireland, which Jubilee was celebrated June 21st 1887.

Thinking it may be of interest in future years and having a little spare time at my disposal I venture to make a few notes from memory, as it will be seen the following account was written nearly 2 years after the events recorded took place. In most of the towns and villages throughout the country the rejoicings were taken up in earnest and feasting, sports, &c were the order of the day. Some of the villages did not observe the Jubilee day proper but had their rejoicings &c at some other day during the summer. In the village of Semington, situate about 3 miles from Trowbridge and 2 miles from Melksham, the following was the programme.

Some time previous a Committee was formed, Mr. W. Bruges being the Chairman, and it was agreed that each villager regardless of their rank or position should have a joint of Beef, the proportion to each family being 2 lb each to the Heads of the family, that is, Husband and Wife, and 1 lb each for the children, or any one who was in the house at the time. Our Household, consisting of myself and wife, the joint that fell to our share was 4 lbs. Two families, at least, received 13 lb each family, the number of their respective Households being the parents and 9 children. The meat was delivered to each house the previous morning or as soon as it could be done on the 20th June. On the following day all the women and children were invited to a free tea and afterwards various sports were indulged in for which prizes were given to the amount of £11.0s. About 220 sat down to Tea, I.H. Stockwell, having contracted to supply the same at 6d. per head. The whole of the expenses were met by the Committee, who had canvassed the village, the inhabitants subscribing liberally to a general fund. A band could not be got on that day for money as so many were wanted in other places, but a Piano was engaged for dancing, but was not much of an attraction. The one mile flat race was won as follows:

1st Charles Watts
2nd William Watts
3rd Thomas Dallimore

A Menagerie Race for Ladies Only caused much amusement, the prizewinners being:

1st Miss Cottle with a Gosling
2nd Mrs Stockwell with a Bantam Cock

There were other entries for this race but the animals, including a pet Lamb and a Rabbit, refused to start.

During the day a Medal was presented to each Child and the whole affair was a complete success, and I may here remark that after every claim was met there remained in the hands of the Treasurer the sum of £3.00. This was kept for a year and on June 6th 1888 all the village children between 3 and 13 years of age [were given Tea?] the Committee again gave the catering into my hands and I think I gave satisfaction.

In the village of Marston, near Devizes, a sheep was roasted, a band was engaged, trees were planted to commemorate the event and a jolly day was spent.

The matter was also taken up in the Towns but by what I read in the papers they did not do it on the same scale as the villages. There was scarcely a village in Wiltshire which did not provide a good feed for the villagers: sometimes it took the shape of a good dinner, in other villages a sheep was roasted and as you will see by my report the village of Semington was provided with meat to cook at their own homes.

In the Town of Melksham a Bullock was roasted, not on the 21st but about a week later. It was placed before a large fire in the Market Place at 4 a.m. and was some hours in cooking, but when it was done people brought their plates and the carver had a busy time of it. My uncle, James Usher, took a very active part in the ox business. In the evening a huge bonfire was lighted in the Market Place which lit up the surrounding buildings. A Band played and those who felt disposed, danced around the fire. The summer of 1887 was hot and dry so that it was an advantage to those who were bent on enjoying themselves. Perhaps I may give you some other chapter at a future time.

There is one item which I had almost forgotten, respecting the Town of Trowbridge. A magnificent Town Hall was built by W. R. Brown, Esq. to commemorate the Jubilee, which is to be opened on June 14 1889 by H.R.H. Princess Louise, Marchioness of Lorre.

God save the Queen and also Henry James Stockwell.

CELEBRATIONS FOR THE GOLDEN JUBILEE OF QUEEN ELIZABETH II IN SEMINGTON ON 3 JUNE 2002

At the beginning of 2002 it was suggested that Semington should celebrate the Queen's Golden Jubilee. Representatives of village organisations and interested individuals were invited to a meeting - about twenty people attended, with ideas on what they thought would appeal to the different age groups, and a programme was drawn up.

It was a brilliant idea by members of the Social Club to suggest a Duck Race on Semington Brook to finance the festivities. Initially 500 ducks were bought and tickets at £1 each were sold, but demand was so great that an extra 200 ducks were obtained. This enabled the activities, competitions, refreshments, etc., to be provided free to all the villagers.

The day began with a Special Jubilee Service at 9.30 a.m. at St George's Church, then at 2 p.m. the afternoon's events got under way in St George's School field. There were four competitions: Putting, the Penalty Shoot-out, Netball Goals and Welly-Wanging. At 2.30 p.m. the races started: the Egg and Spoon Race, the Sack Race, two Tugs of War - one for the children and one for men - the Obstacle Race, three Flat Races and the Water Relay Race. Fortunately the weather was kind until near the end of the afternoon when there was a short downpour just after the Water Relay Race had ended, but this did not last long enough to spoil the proceedings. The Sports Afternoon was great fun, with a lovely atmosphere and very well organised. Everyone involved, including the ladies from the W.I., who had provided tea, cakes and coffee throughout, worked really hard to make it a success and should be congratulated for their efforts.

Other competitions were for the Best Decorated Window and the Best Decorated Bicycle.

Above: Children arrive for party

Left: Welcome speech

After a Parade down through the village from the school field to the Somerset Arms, the younger village children sang a few topical songs composed by several members of St George's School. They were then led inside to a fine feast provided by the landlady, Rebecca Keeble. All the children had plenty to eat and the leftovers were readily consumed by the adults who had poured into the hostelry for a liquid tea.

At 6.15 p.m. the ducks were released over the side of the bridge in a dramatic tumble downwards. As each one hit the water it turned upside down and started its voyage to the finish line. Slowly it became apparent that only the strongest duck would make it to the end of the race. There were many hazards along the way to entrap the ducks. The most difficult obstacle to overcome was the weir. This innocent-looking drop hid a dreadful fate. As each duck skipped over the weir it became stuck in the frothy, turbulent maelstrom. The crowd leaned forward to see which one would regain the open water first, then a roar went up as one plucky little duck bravely fought the current and headed off down the brook. As several others managed to break free it became apparent that as they rounded the bend they would have to steer a middle course to stand any hope of reaching the finish line, and the majority were ensnared by more reeds. The winner of the £50 prize was Kevin Lockwood and 19 others received prizes of £10 each.

Around 6.30 p.m. people began arriving at the Village Hall for the B.B.Q. The servers were kept busy for the next two or three hours selling burgers and hotdogs plus jelly and ice cream. There were outdoor skittles and inside the hall there was singing and occasional disco interludes. As the evening continued the lounge bar was filling up with club members and friends. The bar staff were fully occupied serving Jubilee Beer at £1 a pint and wine at 50 p. a glass. By midnight the barrels were empty and the food was gone.

Monday June 3 was a day to remember. It was good to have so many people willing to make the day a success by running the different events, with so many of the villagers turning out to support it. Special thanks are due to the following people who helped to make the day so memorable:

Sports Afternoon — Suzanne Gilbert (Head Teacher) for the use of St George's School
Bev and Jack Woodward, with all their helpers
Alison Heal and her W.I. ladies
Muriel Woolmington (Judge for Bicycle Competition)

Street Party — Becky and John Keeble (Somerset Arms) and helpers
W.I. ladies

Duck Race — John Allum
Kevin "Donald Duck" Lockwood
Jack Woodward
Tony Rosling
Dave Weston
John Masters, for the use of his field

Village Hall Mac Bennett and the Social Club Committee

Administration Gerald Taylor and Angela Weston
Georgina Collins (Window Competition)
Emma Jackson (Flyers)
Stuart Taylor (Designing/Printing - Certificates and Posters)
(Producing the Jubilee Book)

References

1 Liveing, the Rev. Henry, *The Records of Romsey Abbey*, Winchester: 1906.

2 Gover, J.E.B., Mawer, A., and Stenton, F., *The Place Names of Wiltshire*, 1939, Cambridge University Press, p. 135: 1939.

3 Liveing, the Rev. Henry, *The Records of Romsey Abbey*, Winchester: 1906.

4 Crowley, D.A. (Ed.), *A Wiltshire Tax List of 1332*, Wiltshire Record Society: 1989.

5 Romsey, G.D. (Ed.), 'Two Taxation Lists of 1545 and 1576', Devizes, Wiltshire Archaeological and Natural History Society, Volume X: 1956.

6 Gover, J., Mawer, A., and Stenton, F., *The Place Names of Wiltshire*, Cambridge University Press, p. 143: 1939.

7 Information from *Victoria County History: Wiltshire*, Volume VIII, Section on Whorwellsdown.

8 Pafford, J.H.P. (Ed.), 'Accounts of the Parliamentary Garrisons of Great Chalfield and Marlborough 1645-1646', WANHS Vol. II p. 47.

9 Wiltshire Buildings Record - WRO B.1968.

See also Wroughton, J., *An Unhappy Civil War*, Bath, The Lansdown Press: 1999.

10 Information from *Victoria County History: Wiltshire*, Volume VII, pp. 7-14.

St. George's Church, north side

Chapter 2

THE CHURCHES

St GEORGE'S CHURCH

It would be impossible to consider the early history of Semington without reference to Steeple Ashton - now a large village but once a small market town which owed its prosperity, and its magnificent 15th century Church of St Mary the Virgin, to the cloth trade, until a fire destroyed many of the houses. In Saxon times the Manor of Ashton, including the surrounding villages of Great Hinton, Semington, West Ashton, North Bradley and Southwick, was owned by King Edgar (959-975) who bequeathed it to the Abbess of Romsey. Thereafter the nuns held the whole estate until the Dissolution of the monasteries, when it was acquired by Thomas, Lord Seymour of Sudeley. When he was executed for treason in 1549 it passed to the Crown. Various people seem to have owned parts of Semington after that but by the late 18th century much of the village was in the ownership of the Duke of Somerset.

One of the earliest pieces of information to be found regarding Semington is a Charter[1], now in the Manuscript Collections of the British Library, dated 28 May 1470, concerning a "difference" which had arisen between twenty parishioners and other inhabitants of "Semyngton & Litilton" of the one part and Thomas Waget, vicar of "Stepulasshton" of the other part, the complainants alleging that the Vicar was bound to provide a Chaplain to celebrate holy services, etc., in the Chapel of St George in the hamlet of "Semyngton" and the Vicar denying his liability. The decision was left to the Bishop, Richard Beauchamp, who decreed that the Vicar should provide a Chaplain for the celebration of Mass and Evensong in the said Chapel on all Sundays and holy days, including burial(all churches at that time being Roman Catholic), and that the inhabitants should, in addition to the usual tithes, etc., due by custom, pay the Vicar twenty shillings a year by half yearly payments at the feast of St John the Baptist and at Christmas.

Semington is therefore an ancient Chapelry. The official title of the Benefice in the Bishop's Book at the Diocesan Registry is Steeple Ashton cum Semington. The Church, or officially, Chapel, at Semington had its own Registers, which date from 1586. From the 16th century until 1939 there was a Curate-in-Charge, who was expected to reside in Semington, which had its own Vestry (or management committee) and its own Chapel wardens with independent Minute book and Accounts. It had its own Vestry Clerk who took the fees due to that office. It still has its own Church of England School and its own Charities, the distribution of which is a matter for the Semington Chapelry alone.[2]

The Church (or Chapel) is dedicated to St George. Some of the stones in the building go back to Norman times. The nave and porch are of the 15th century and the chancel of the first part of the 16th. Built into the porch is a stone with an incised inscription in old French, probably dating from the 13th century, the translation of which is: "Whoever shall say a Pater Noster and an Ave Maria for the souls of Philippa de Sale and Christians, shall have forty days of pardon".[3]

Until recently the Ten Commandments were writ large on the walls on each side of the stained glass windows behind the altar, but they are at present obscured.

The office of Church or Chapelwarden goes back a long way but few early records have survived. In Steeple Ashton the Churchwardens' Accounts began in 1543, when it was noted that "The churchewardyns of Semyngton payeth to the church yerely at ester xs vd (10s. 5d.). Apart from noting fairly regularly as the years go by that this amount had been received (or not, as the case might be). There is very little mention of Semington in the Steeple Ashton records.

The terms "vestry" and "vestry meeting" appear to have evolved in the 16th century or earlier as a kind of parish parliament, with the minister, the churchwardens and the leading parishioners meeting once a year to inspect and approve the churchwardens' accounts (which listed the monies spent during the previous year), to levy a tax on those who could pay and to elect the wardens for a further year. The office of warden could be somewhat burdensome, but it was difficult to avoid. Every householder in the village was expected to serve for a year as one of the parish officers, or to provide a substitute Anyone who declined the honour could be fined heavily and until 1964 common law compelled any warden to accept the office, which was unpaid. One exemption was by "Tyburn Ticket", a written document signed

13th century stone

Church Pulpit

3238-59
Record of a conviction before the Assizes of Joshua Scamp for horse theft in Steeple Ashton endorsed with an assignment. John Marsh the victim and captor of Scamp of his Tyburn Ticket to Thomas Bruges.
Scamp was a gipsy whose grave in Odstock became a place of pilgrimage to travelling people because of his fortitude in protecting his son-in-law, the actual thief.

WILTS
These are to Certify that at the General Gaol Delivery held at New Sarum and for the County of Wilts on Saturday the Seventh day of March Instant before me whose name is hereunto subscribed one of His Majesty's Justices Assigned to deliver the Gaol of the County aforementioned of the Prisoners therein being Joshua Shemp otherwise Scamp was Tried and Convicted of feloniously stealing on the Fifth day of October last at The Parish of Steeple Ashton one Gelding of the price of Three Pounds the property of John Marsh and that it doth appear to me that the said John Marsh did apprehend and take the same Joshua Shemp otherwise Scamp and did prosecute him until he was Convicted of the Felony and Horsestealing aforesaid and that for a Reward unto the said John Marsh upon such Conviction by virtue of an Act of Parliament made in the tenth and eleventh years of the Reign of His Late Majesty King William the Third Intitled an Act for the better apprehending prosecuting and punishing of Felons that Commit Burglary Housebreaking or Robbery in Shops Warehouses Coachhouses or Stables or that Steal Horses the said John Marsh ought to be and is discharged of and from all manner of Parish and Ward Offices within the Parish of Steeple Ashton aforesaid wherein the Felony and Horsestealing aforesaid was Committed And this I do hereby Certify in order to his being discharged accordingly. Given under my Hand this Tenth day of March one thousand eight Hundred and one.

A THOMSON

ON REVERSE OF DOCUMENT:
The within named John Marsh Do hereby assign transfer and set over all my Right Title and Interest benefit and advantages of the within Certificate unto Thomas Bruges of Semington in the parish of Steeple Ashton in the County of Wilts Gentleman Witness my hand this 25th day of April 1801

JOHN MARSH

WITNESS: THOS. TIMBRELL JNR

Transcription of 'Tyburn Ticket' from Bruges Family Papers in Wiltshire Record Office by a Justice of the Peace, confirming that the holder, by virtue of apprehending a criminal and bringing him (or her) to justice, had been rewarded by being relieved from all parochial duties. This Ticket was transferable; and could fetch up to £20.[4] A rare example exists in the Bruges Family Papers[5] in the WRO, a transcription of which is on the preceding page.

Semington's Chapelwardens' Accounts date from 1744, with Maurice Jarvis as Chapelwarden.. A copy of his Accounts for that year will be found on the next page, from which it will be seen that £9.14s.10d. had been expended for a variety of purposes and that a tax had been levied on four parishioners for his reimbursement - leaving a "Ballance" of 2d. to be carried over to the following year. Churchwardens' duties included attending the Bishop at Visitations, providing bread and wine for communion, arranging for the parish registers to be copied and sent to the Bishop, paying for maintenance of the chapel, giving money to the poor, and paying villagers who brought them the remains of such animals as otters, foxes, pole cats, etc., then regarded as pests. The vestry "clark" received 4 shillings (a year!).

By 1755 there were two Chapelwardens and others who attended the Vestry Meeting were:

A.. Awdry
Edmond Lowis
Thos. Bruges
Wm. Beavan

Left: Church Font
Above: "Skull & Crossbones tomb"

1744The Parish of Semington to Maurice Jarvis by Disbursements in the office of Chapell Warden

Sworn in at the Prianneall Visitation at Devizes September 1744

Sept. 7	To Robt Mattick late Chappell Warden	£4 12 9
	To the Presentment	13 6
	To Fees	4 6
	To Expences at Visitation	1 6
	Pd for a Fox	1
June 5	To Wine and Bread	3 1
28	Pd for two Otters	1
Dec 14	To Expenses at Visitation	4 6
	To the Presentment	2 6
	To the Apparitor	1 6
	To the Kings Tax and Receipts	4
	To the Revd Mr Thompson	1 10
	To the Clark	4
	To the Poor	12
		£9 14 10
Per Contra		
Apl 15	By Cash by Mr Drinkwater	£3
	By do Mr Lowis	1
	By do Robt. Mattick	3 5
	By do Mr Brooks	2 10
		£9 15
		£9 14 10
	Dr to Ballance	2

NOTES

Presentment: Statement made on oath by a churchwarden at a bishop's Visitation.

Visitation: Official visit of bishop to inspect the churches of his diocese.

Apparitor An officer of an ecclesiastical court who summoned people to appear before it

Prianneall This word does not appear in the *Oxford English Dictionary* but presumably it refers to the fact that the Visitations occurred twice a year.

Transcript from Semington Chapelwarden's accounts. WRO 714/18

In 1757 the names of four different people signed as having attended the Vestry and these were joined by Isaac Gulliver and Henry Gale, who could not sign but made their marks. Possibly this Isaac Gulliver was the father of Isaac, the celebrated and notorious smuggler of Dorset, who was said to have been born in 1745 in Semington. Certainly the baptism of one "Isaac Gulifor" "the son of Elizabeth and Isaac" is recorded in Semington Parish Register[5] on 29 September 1745. An Isaac Gulliver again appears at the Vestry Meeting in 1766 and in 1767 was renting the field called "Downfield" from the Chapel Charity lands (perhaps enjoying the proceeds from his son's activities?)

From 1770 onwards a member of the Bruges family became one of the two Chapelwardens. First, there was Thomas, from 1770 to 1782, then William, from 1783 to 1831 (he obviously did not take advantage of the "Tyburn Ticket" given to him in 1801) then Thomas from 1849 to 1880, then William from 1891 to 1912. In 1927 Mr C. Ernest Bruges took over until 1957. After his death his widow remained a member of the Parochial Church Council. It would appear that members of the Bruges family were either involved with the Church or maintained one of the offices of Chapelwarden of Semington almost without a break until 1999, when Major Michael Bruges stepped down as Chapelwarden, although retaining the office of Treasurer of St George's Church until he and Mrs Tara Bruges left the village in 2001.

The eighteenth century accounts show that in 1746 the expenses included "To Form of prayers during the Rebellion - 2s. 6d." "To Order of Council for preventing distemper among Cattle - 2s. 6d." "To two Otters and One Fox - 3s.", In 1754: "Gave to som saylors 6d.", In 1755: "To 8 Seamen and Woman three Children 1s.6d." "To 38 dozen of Sparrow Heads - 6s.4d."[6]

As the years went by more people were involved in the Vestry Meetings and by 1770 they were attended by the agent for the Duke of Somerset, a confirmation that by that time the Duke owned much of the land. The Tithe Map of 1837 shows well over twenty landowners, including All Souls College, Oxford, a number of clergymen, Walter Long and, of course, His Grace the Duke of Somerset (who sold most of his property in the village soon after the Second World War).

There appears to have been a Curate-in-Charge at Semington (appointed either by the Bishop of Salisbury or the Vicar of Steeple Ashton) since the 14th century. There is in existence an Indenture (or agreement between several parties) dated 1597 regarding "Semington Chapel Lands Charity" which set aside certain lands and tenements in Semington for the maintenance of the Chapel and the relief of the poor of Semington and Littleton, to be managed by a number of "feoffees" or trustees. By 1683 the "sundrie other good and charitable purposes" seem to have extended to the building of a tenement "commonly called or knowne by the name of the Church house" . In 1704 it was said that a room in this house (which was in fact next to St George's Chapel) was let to the Curate. In 1833 it is described as an old thatched dwelling which was let to the Overseers of the Poor.[7] In the 1841 Census Return this house was lived in by an agricultural labourer and his family.

Then the dwelling on the land between Church Street and the High Street, which became known as "The Parsonage" must have been built. It was certainly occupied in 1851 by the Reverend Henry Crawley, his wife, two daughters and two servants, and by all subsequent Curates and their families until the house was sold to the Red Cross in the 1960s.

According to Canon Knubley (pictured left, courtesy *Wiltshire Times*), writing some time in the 1930s, Semington Parsonage had been the property of Mr William Bruges, who let it to the Vicar of Steeple Ashton for the use of the Curate-in-Charge at a rental of £27 per annum. On Mr Bruges' death the house was put up to Auction in May 1923 and was bought by Mr C. Ernest Bruges for £760. He then put it in thorough repair at a cost of £100 and gave it to his daughter, Margaret Joan Bruges, who let it to the Vicar of Steeple Ashton for £45 a year.[8] No earlier information regarding the erection of this house has yet been found.

A sad story is told about one of the Curates of Semington, William Wainhouse. He fell in love with Anne Beach, daughter of the Lord of the Manor of Keevil, and she with him.[9] Her parents did not approve, and kept Anne in solitary confinement in a room at Keevil Manor for a whole year. When she would not change her mind they relented, and William and Anne were married. Sadly, Anne died shortly afterwards, in 1771, in her twenty-second year. There is a memorial to her in Steeple Ashton Church.

By 1858 the Vestry Clerk was being paid £5.5s. a year and his duties included arranging for the washing of surplices, cleaning the chapel yard and the chapel windows, weeding the churchyard and providing bread for the sacrament. In 1875 William Dallimore was engaged as Clerk at an annual salary of £8. He continued in the office until 1910, when he resigned owing

Left: Anne Beach Memorial

Above: Church Vestry

to advancing age and increasing infirmity. In 1911 George Ritchens took over at a salary of £9.

Every year since the 18th century, when the Chapelwardens presented their accounts, they were repaid partly through the rents from the chapel lands and partly from "Semington Chapel Lands Charity", mentioned earlier, which was still being administered by a number of trustees. If any special expenditure was required for repairs to the chapel, or as in 1877, for the building of a new Vestry, (a small room in which the vestments are kept), the amount was raised by subscription, the trustees still contributing anything to make up the difference.

An Account Book headed "Semington Chapel Charity" and dated from 1829 notes that in 1830 £56.11s6d. was paid to enable Mary Hill and her 10 children, likewise George Wheeler, to emigrate to New York. They were followed in 1832 by Elizabeth, wife of George Bendy, and her five children and in 1842 by James Sainsbury, his wife and eight children, costing £27.16s.3d. It would be interesting to know whether any of them survived, and where their descendants are!

By the beginning of the 20th century things were beginning to change: the Parish Council had been formed in 1894, taking over some of the duties formerly undertaken by the chapelwardens. The Curate seems not to have attended the Vestry Meetings after 1910: these were subsequently chaired by Canon Knubley, Vicar of Steeple Ashton until he retired in 1931. In January 1925 the Parochial Church Council was formed. Since then the Vestry Meetings have still been held every year, in April, and the churchwardens are still nominated and elected before the beginning of the Annual Church Meeting which takes place in the presence of the parishioners. Only those on the church electoral roll are entitled to vote and to approve the Annual Accounts, now presented by the Treasurer.

During the 1960s Anglican and Methodist co-operation in the Parish was being discussed and suggestions were being made that there should be shared services in both the Anglican Church and the Wesleyan Chapel. By 1971 the vicar was the Reverend A. R. Moore and Keevil parish had been added to Steeple Ashton and Semington. These extra responsibilities meant that the Vicar had to cope with three different churches every Sunday!

St. George's Church, south side

During this time the Wesleyan Chapel was sold (see section on the Wesleyan Chapel) and in September 1981 St George's Anglican Parochial Church Council combined with Semington Methodist Church Council to allow for the joint use of St George's Church for both Methodist and Anglican services. Subsequently St George's Joint Parochial Church Council was formed, which includes Anglican and Methodist members and meets regularly three or four times a year to consider matters concerning their joint interests.

During the year 2000 St George's became, with the Bishop's approval, an independent parish within the benefice and can now legally be known as St George's Church.

WORLD WAR I (1914-1918)	**WORLD WAR II** (1939-1945)
R.W. BUTLER	N.A. FARR
H.B. FISHER	F.B. FLOWER
W.H. FORSYTH	W.L. KEMP
F.C. GULLIVER	C.H. TITT
F.L. MOORE	E.C. WATTS
A.C. PERRETT	
G.H. SWAINE	**KOREAN WAR** (1951)
C.F. WHEELER	W. ADAIR

Roll of honour: *As recorded in St. George's Church and on the War Memorial in the Churchyard.*

THE PARISH OF SEMINGTON.

Eric Hancock.

1939. 1945.

The Parishioners of Semington herewith desire to recognise sincerely the sacrifices made and services rendered the Nation and Humanity during the Second World War by presenting this Certificate with a small gift of money to those who went out from the Parish and others, who became connected with it during that time, to the exclusion of similar recognition from another source.

Whilst gifts and words are limited, the gratitude and appreciation are unbounded and unfailing.

We rejoice in your safe return after taking part in the final success which was never in doubt even in the darkest days.

The village suffered grievous losses, and we proudly and sympathetically honour the memory of Norman A. Farr, and those others who had family ties with members of our community who paid the supreme sacrifice.

Signed Joseph Hoad
(Chairman of Welcome Home Committee).

Florence E. Farr
(Secretary).

Adelaide A. Bolwell
(Treasurer).

Welcome Home certificate (courtesy Mrs J Fry).

THE WESLEYAN CHAPEL

The "Compton Census" of 1676 (named after Henry Compton, Bishop of London) was one of the earliest census returns in this country and is a major source for estimating the size of local populations, although it only recorded people over the age of 16. Semington at that time is shown as having 207 "conformists" (or Anglicans) and 2 "non-conformists".[10]

Houses were licensed for Methodist meetings in Steeple Ashton and Semington in 1797 and in 1829 the Methodists of Semington had 27 members and an average congregation of 80.[11]

There is a document in Wiltshire Record Office dated 1st September 1819 regarding an Assignment by Mr Robert Wilshire to Mr Samuel Beaven and others of "a piece of Ground at Semington for the purpose of building a Chapel thereon". The Licence for this Chapel is dated 25th April 1819, and the Indenture mentioned above was signed and sealed in the presence of Samuel Beaven Jnr on 21 January 1820.[12] It was not, however, until 1884 that application was made by the Reverend James Waller, of Bradford-on-Avon, and Messrs John Linzey, James John Hibberd and Edward Watts for consent to the erection of a chapel and vestry at Semington at a cost of £301,including purchase of land, cost towards its lighting, warming, furnishing, etc., architect's commission and all other expenses. This was sanctioned by the Wesleyan Committee, Manchester, on 31 May, 1884.[13]

Early view of Chapel. (Courtesy Mrs M. Gover)

The fact that the Chapel was built at this time seems to have had much to do with the arrival in Semington in 1884 of the new sub-Postmaster and grocer, Mr Henry James Stockwell, an active Wesleyan, who was known throughout the area for his devotion to the cause. For the next 50 years, until his death in 1935, Mr Stockwell was involved in all the public works in the village: he was clerk to the Parish Council for 39 years and Chairman of the Committee responsible for the building of the Village Hall. His involvement with Methodism included Trustee of the Trowbridge and Bradford Circuit, Chapel Steward, Superintendent of the Sunday School, and organist. His wife, Mrs Adelaide Stockwell, was also a very active Methodist and, as a shopkeeper with her husband, was much concerned with life in the village.

Methodist Outing (courtesy Mrs M. Gover).

In 1912 the Duke of Somerset gave some land to enable a room for a Sunday School to be built attached to the Chapel. It was recorded in *The Wiltshire Times* on 5th October 1912 that the new Sunday School was in the process of being erected, for 80 scholars, and the memorial stones had been laid by Mrs Stockwell, Miss Bowyer, Miss Lomas, Miss Bailey, Mrs Farr and Mrs Noad. Tea had been served later, in Mr Bishop's carpenter's shop.

Gradually during the 20th century, as the village grew in size, the congregations of both the Anglican and Methodist churches did not increase in proportion. Eventually it seemed more appropriate to have one place of worship rather than two. In 1981 the Methodist Church Council agreed to the sale of the Wesleyan Chapel and the last service was held on 13th September.[14] The then Methodist congregation rejoiced in the kind invitation from the Anglican community to share the Church Building in a Local Ecumenical Project and the inaugural joint service with the Church of England was held on Sunday 27th September. After 30th December 1981 all further meetings of the Parochial Church Council included members of the Methodist Church Council and it has since been termed "The Joint Parochial Church Council, St George's, Semington".

We have rejoiced in God's love ever since in enabling Free Church witness, with joyous 10th and 20th Church Sharing Anniversaries. The work of God in mission and outreach continues to prosper as we share His love for each one of us, as we proclaim His Glory in a non-labelling denominational environment.

The Methodist Chapel building became a private house. It was sold for £12,234, which amount was sent to the Circuit Advance Fund.

SEMINGTON SUNDAY SCHOOL

Mrs Betty Bennett, then Betty Baker, had been going to Sunday School since she was 5 years old, when it was being run by a Miss Violet Ritchens. During the War (in 1942) when she was still quite young, Betty was told there was a vacancy for a Sunday School teacher and was asked whether she would like to take over. She agreed, and with the help of her sister, presided over the Sunday School, which was held in the Church at 2.30 every Sunday

The children sang hymns and had readings and stories from the Bible. Sometimes they had outings to Steeple Ashton , where they could have races and play games and then have tea. Another treat was when they went to Mrs Robinson's cottage in Stoggy Lane, which had a lovely garden with a paddling pool and also an old 'roundabout' which all the children loved.

Mrs Bennett's involvement with the Sunday School lasted for over 40 years and only ceased in 1995, because of the dwindling attendances. At the Church Fete in 1996 she was presented with a glass bowl to mark her years of service.

Records of an Anglican Sunday School in Semington go back to 1799, when the school was paid for by subscriptions from about ten of the more important inhabitants. Later these included the Duke of Somerset, Walter Long, Esq. and the Vicar of Steeple Ashton. Some of the school registers still exist in Wiltshire Record Office. In 1810 there were 14 boys and 17 girls on the register although there were many absences, particularly at harvest time.

St. GEORGE'S CHURCH CHOIR

In September 1947, before the Harvest Festival Service, several of the local lads were asked if they would sit up at the front of the Church, instead of their usual place at the back, and help with the singing.

This was further investigated and the choir cassocks and surplices, which had not been used for several years, were washed and cleaned, tried and fitted, and used once again.

In 1970, with the choir going strong and now including women for the first time, it was decided to ask for donations from the village and local businesses to purchase new purple cassocks for the choir members. These were dedicated at Easter, 1970, together with a red cassock for the cross bearer. The cross and the red cassock were a gift from the late Reverend H R Cattarns, who was a very popular visiting preacher for several years.

This choir held a reunion in 1997, 50 years after it had begun. Some members are still active today.

From Mac Bennett (one of the originals and Church organist for 46 years).

Choir Outing, 1951. (Courtesy Mrs P. Mortimer)

References

1 From information given to Canon Knubley by the Diocesan Registrar, Salisbury. The document in question is in the Manuscript Collections of the British Library. Its full reference is "British Library Additional Charter 5691"

2 From Canon Knubley's "Diary Notes", courtesy of Mrs Betty Smith, of Steeple Ashton

3 Victoria County History: Wiltshire, Volume VIII, p. 215

4 Tate, W.E., *The Parish Chest*, p. 23

5 From The Parish Registers & Bishops Transcripts of Semington, transcribed by Wiltshire Family History Society, 1989/1992

6 Semington Chapelwardens' Accounts WRO 714/18

7 *VCH Wiltshire*, Vol. VIII p. 213

8 From Canon Knubley's "Diary Notes" as above

9 Rogers, Kenneth, *Steeple Ashton: Village History and Guide* 1986, p. 20. Published by The Friends of Steeple Ashton

10 *Wiltshire Notes & Queries* Vol. III p. 537

11 *VCH Wiltshire* Vol. VIII p. 216

12 WRO 1904/1

13 WRO 1904/13

14 WRO 2587/28

Wesleyan Chapel

In the middle of this terrace lived the village blacksmith. The funeral bier is still kept there

No. 10 High Street, postcard view dated 28 May 1910. (Courtesy Mrs M. Gover)

High Street

Chapter 3

POPULATION, OCCUPATIONS AND HOUSING

The General Register Office was created in 1836, and was responsible for the recording of births, marriages and deaths and for the collecting of census returns, commencing with the Census of 1841. The first census for the whole of Britain had been taken in 1801 but no local material survives, nor from those of 1811, 1821, and 1831, and that for 1841 is very difficult to read. Therefore before the middle of the nineteenth century it is difficult to estimate the total population of a village such as Semington. One method is by the use of the various tax returns which have survived. For instance, the Wiltshire Tax List of 1332[1] records the names of 22 men in Semington (Sembletone) who paid taxes varying from 5s. 3¼d. to 8d. Taxes were levied on people who owned property, so this may mean that there were at least 22 houses in the village at that time.

Both Henry VIII and Elizabeth I used taxes to fund their wars. In 1545 there was one person in Littleton and four men in "Semyngton" who paid anything from 40s. to 10s. as a "benevolence, or loving contribution" to Henry - a total of £5; and Elizabeth's "Subsidy" of 1576 for the "Tething of Semyngton and Litelton" produced £62 and £10. 5s .2d. in two instalments (of 2s8d in the £ and 16d. in the £) from nine people.[2]

Bishop Compton's "Ecclesiastical Census" of 1676, taken to estimate the number of "Conformists" and "Non-conformists" in each Parish, showed Semington as having 207 Conformists and 2 Nonconformists. This total of 209 only included adults over 16, so it can be estimated that the total population was in the region of 334.[3]

There is in Wiltshire Record Office a list of names of people living in Semington in 1800 (including Littlemarsh, Ragged Smock, Strangers Corner, Penny Platt, Littleton Wood, Patience Mill and Paxcroft). Against each name is a number, which is presumed to be the number of people actually living in the same house as the person named (in later census returns shown as "head of household"). From this list it can be assumed that at that time the population was 253, or 292 with Paxcroft.[4] In 1813 the Vicar of Steeple Ashton also made a list, of his own parish and of Semington, which showed the population of Semington as 259.[5]

In the Baptism and Burial Registers from St George's Chapel in Semington,[6] the earliest indication of any trades in the village is in the 1590s, when a clothier and a farmer are mentioned. Later, in 1622, a blacksmith named Phillipe Tucker was buried at the church. By the early 19th century Semington had both butchers and bakers, but, unfortunately, there is no mention of a candlestick maker. There were also tanners, shoemakers, carpenters, wheelwrights and, because of the opening of the Kennet and Avon and the Wiltshire and Berkshire canals, there were boatmen, boatbuilders, lock keepers, a wharfinger (owner or manager of a wharf) and a Clerk of the Wharf living in Semington.[7]

It was not until the 1841 census that occupations were included on the forms and it would appear that there were only 34 houses and 173 people living in the village at that time. These included 4 farmers, 18 agricultural labourers, 1 nurse, 1 governess, 3 carpenters, 1 maltster, 1 tailor, 1 police constable and 1 blacksmith. 13 other men and women were employed as servants.

By the time of the 1851 census there were 90 houses in the parish of Semington, which now included Littlemarsh, Littleton and Strangers Corner. The population had nearly doubled to 303, not counting the inmates of Melksham Union Workhouse. With the increased population came more varied occupations, not only butchers and bakers but coopers, shoemakers, cattle and horse dealers, harness makers, dressmakers, a seamstress and a laundress. There was also a

Wartime family, 1914-18.
(Courtesy Mrs J. Fry)

railway worker, who might have worked on the Westbury to Thingley line which passed through Holt. For the first time brick and tile workers are recorded, who possibly worked at the Semington Brickyard, near Brickfield Farm. In the little red brick cottage near Semington Roundabout (then Semington Crossroads) lived Emily Springform, the Turnpike Collector. Semington House employed six servants. There was also a fuller (a person who treats and prepares cloth) and 39 children are recorded as being scholars, together with one schoolmistress.

Mrs June Fry's mother and aunt. (Courtesy Mrs J. Fry)

In the 1861 census there were 63 houses and 251 people registered as living in Semington. The fluctuations in the number of houses and the number of people living in the village since 1851 were probably due to parish boundary changes. Agriculture dominated the lives of most of the inhabitants at that time. Manor Farm employed 13 men, 4 boys and 4 women. Church Farm employed 4 men and 1 boy, and 5 men and 1 boy worked at Paxcroft Farm. Canal work had now finished but 4 men and 2 boys were employed at the brickworks at Penny Platt. At the Parsonage, at the corner of Church Street and the High Street, lived Charles Down, aged 36, who was the new Curate, with his wife and three young sons. Also living in Semington at that time was Mr Henry Vagg, aged 76, a Chelsea Pensioner, with his 43 year old wife and their two children aged 9 and 3 respectively. Although at that time there were 53 scholars in Semington no schoolteacher seemed to reside in the village. Thirsts could be quenched at The Somerset Arms or the grey stone building on the opposite side of the road named The Jolly Butcher (later and earlier) called The Bell. The 'Manor House' next to The Somerset Arms now served as Post Office, grocer's shop and bakery.

Church Street prior to 1967 (courtesy Mrs J. Fry).

Church Street.

Church Fête, c. 1948 (courtesy Mrs P Mortimer)

There were 67 houses and 277 people residing in Semington at the 1871 census. Amongst the older generation 14 alms men and women were living on charity. Two men aged 80 still described themselves as labourers. At the other end of the wage scale two 11 year old lads were employed as plough boy and labourer respectively. Families with six or seven children were normal in the mid 19th century. In 1871 Samuel and Elizabeth Watts had a daughter, Louisa, aged 6 years, a son, George, aged 5, a son, William, aged 3 and a son, Charles, aged 1. By the time of the 1881 census there were also sons Albert, aged 9, Edward aged 7, Henry aged 5, Alfred aged 3 and Ernest aged 3 weeks. Ten years later two daughters had joined the family: Mary aged 7 and Elizabeth aged 4.

The 1881 census records 63 houses and 300 people. Among them was another Chelsea Pensionser: Thomas Gulliver. 60 children were shown as scholars, with ages ranging from 3 to 16 years.

Little had changed in the village by 1891. There were 60 houses and 267 people. Ten families were farming in the parish, including Stephen Bailey at Strangers Corner Farm, who was also a veterinary surgeon. Frances Rabbitts was the 23 year old schoolmistress - living with her 12 year old sister in a four-roomed cottage. Although only 12 children were recorded as "scholars" in the census return the school records show that the average attendance was 42 in 1891. Also living in the village were Police Constable George Smith and a 45 year old sculptor and artist, Richard Dyer.

The last census for which the enumerators' books are open to public inspection, that for 1901, shows little difference from that of 1891. 57 houses were canvassed and Littlemarsh, Strangers Corner, Penny Platt. Littleton and Paxcroft Farm were included in the return. There were, however, eight houses unoccupied (including Church Farmhouse, although by then Church Farm and Manor Farm were being run jointly by the Jeffreys brothers). There were 12 farmers, 1 market gardener and 23 people were in some form of employment connected with farming. The sculptor was still in residence, though he had apparently aged 15 years instead of 10 (unfortunately inaccuracies do abound in these early records). As a sign of impending change one individual's occupation is given as "platelayer on railway" and another is "driver, traction engine".

One useful piece of information asked for in the 1851 census and subsequently was the place of birth of each individual, which means that we can tell rather more about the composition of the village for the next 50 years. For instance was this a "closed" village: were "incomers" accepted readily or

Opening of village shop, 1959. (Courtesy Wiltshire Times*)*

not? Did the young men seek wives from other villages rather than from their own? Were there many marriages within the village? Did many young women of the village find husbands from elsewhere, and how many couples arrived in Semington from elsewhere and settled there?

Oddly enough, over the fifty years from 1851 to 1901 the figures remain relatively static as shown in the following table:

CENSUS YEARS	**1851**	**1861**	**1871**	**1881**	**1891**	**1901**
"Head of Household" born in Semington	27	27	22	24	22	23
"Head" born elsewhere	45	34	41	40	38	34
Wife & "Head" born Semington	6	6	5	8	7	3
Wives only born Semington	8	9	8	8	2	1
Wives born elsewhere	50	34	34	33	33	12
Both husband & wife born elsewhere and in same place	4	3	3	3	1	3

During the fifty years from 1851 to 1901 only the Curates, the Postmaster, the Police Constables and those "living on own means" came from any distance. Generally speaking, the "incomers" came from other towns and villages in Wiltshire or Somerset and farming and its associated activities provided employment for most of them, apart from the brickworks and the canals.

Village shop

Of those born in Semington, the same names crop up throughout the years, some even going back to the 1580s, as recorded in the Parish Registers of Baptisms and Burials.

From the National Census figures, the graph on page 50 shows the population of Semington fluctuating between 250 and 300 persons up until the year 1931. The number of inmates in the Workhouse over the same time varied between 150 and 170.

It should be explained here that whilst the full figures from a National Census are not available to the general public for 100 years, a small synopsis giving population and housing totals is normally published within a year of the census being conducted.

By 1951 change was happening: the population rose above 350, an average increase of some 25% after more than a century of stability. In the period 1961-1971 a further rise of approximately 75% occurred. This can be explained by the construction of several small housing estates. The additional housing was just a step (albeit a rather large step) in the expansion of

A=Village + Workhouse / N.H.S. Hospital population.

B=Village population only.

C=Housing Stock.

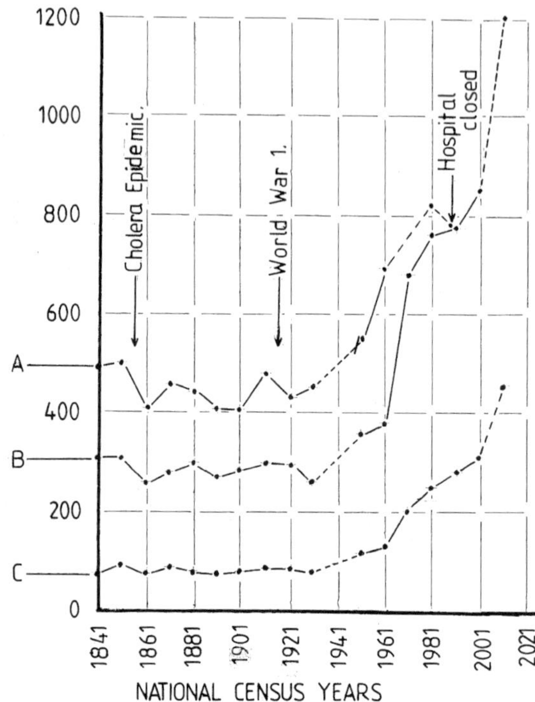

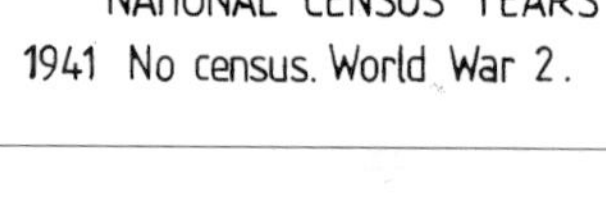

Graph compiled from Census Returns by DMF.

The Knapps

Highfield Close

Pound Close

Somerset Way

Manor Close

Church Street

Church Street

Littlemarsh

The Orchard

Semington, for by the year 1991 more houses had been built, bringing the population up to some 770 persons.

With current and proposed building it may well be that the number of people living in Semington will rise above 1200 by the Census year of 2011.

That the population remained stable for about a century could be attributed to the nature of employment, which was mainly labouring of one kind or another. The change commenced during and after World War II, from 1939 to 1945, when an industrial revolution took place in farming, caused by the introduction of mechanisation, which resulted in fewer people being required to run a farm. The number of labourers employed on a farm of reasonable size at one time might have been some 15 or 16. By the year 2000 farms generally were being run by the family with the use of the occasional contractor or two at peak times, such as harvest.

Obviously this run down in farming employment produced a large number of job seekers and this was attractive to industrial organisations, who sometimes needed employees by the hundred. Some of these companies were also looking to expand and Wiltshire, being a very attractive county for scenery, offered good conditions for working. The influx of organisations coming to the area and also several local companies taking on additional workers had the effect of drawing into the locality even more people looking for work, hence the large increase in the housing stock. The population was also further increased by a large number of retired persons moving to the West of England in search of a pleasant life at a more reasonable pace than in the larger cities.

References

1 See 'A Wiltshire Tax List of 1332', Wiltshire Record Society Vol. XLV (1989)

2 From 'Two Taxation Lists, 1545 and 1576', WANHS Vol. X (1956) pp. 35 and 139

3 "Bishop Compton's Census". See WN&Q Vol. III p. 537

4 WRO 730/288

5 WRO 730/288/3

6 From 'The Parish Registers & Bishops Transcripts of Semington', transcribed by Wiltshire Family History Society 1989/1992

7 See also Semington Census Returns, 1841-1901

Palmer Grove.

Above: Numbers 5 and 5a High Street.

Left: Pound Lane.

Below: St. George's Court.

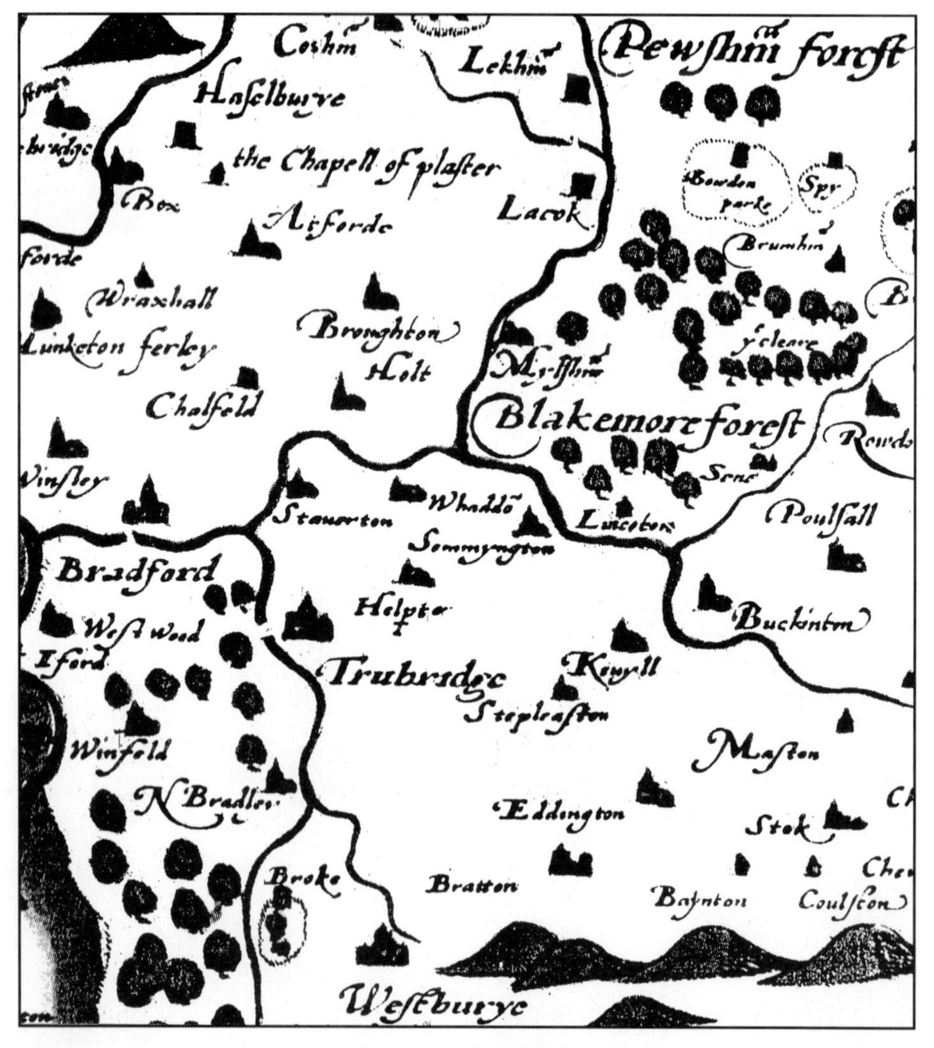

Saxton, 1576. WRO.

Chapter 4

MAPS AND ARCHAEOLOGY

It is difficult if not impossible to determine when drawn travelling instructions were first produced. There must have been some "sketch maps" long before Saxton produced his first "symbol" map of Wiltshire in 1576. The signs were very basic – a church of variant size and shaped as a "likeness" represented a settlement of, say, anything from a village to a city, provided that place did actually have a church. Other places were represented by a house or a tower, if there was no church. Forests were shown by drawings of trees and hills were depicted by shaded "lumps" which bore some resemblance to the actual vertical outline of the hills.

These various symbols were placed on the map in positions closely relating to their places in real life. Names were then added adjacent to the sketches and many of these names can be related to current titles of towns and villages. No connecting routes were shown – the only lines representing rivers.

Jansson in 1646 moved the cartography a step further towards accuracy by including in the symbols a circle which more accurately represented the geographical position of the place named alongside. Jansson also included dotted outlines of the various "hundreds". This work was closely followed in 1689 by Lea, who basically produced an upgraded version of Saxton's map, but included the "hundreds" and the Devizes/Trowbridge/Farleigh Castle road passing through "Semmyngton".

In 1791 Tunnicliff produced a map which could be regarded as the forerunner to the Ordnance Survey map with which we are familiar today. Roads are drawn between settlements, some miniature sketches of churches are included to denote the larger towns and the spellings are basically those of today.

The next available map of the area was in 1793, by the brothers Whitworth who, as engineers, produced work for the design of the Wilts and Berks Canal. An interesting feature is the suggestion for the junction with the Kennet and Avon Canal, with a second, more westward, additional link which obviously

Jansson, 1646. WRO.

Lea, 1689. WRO.

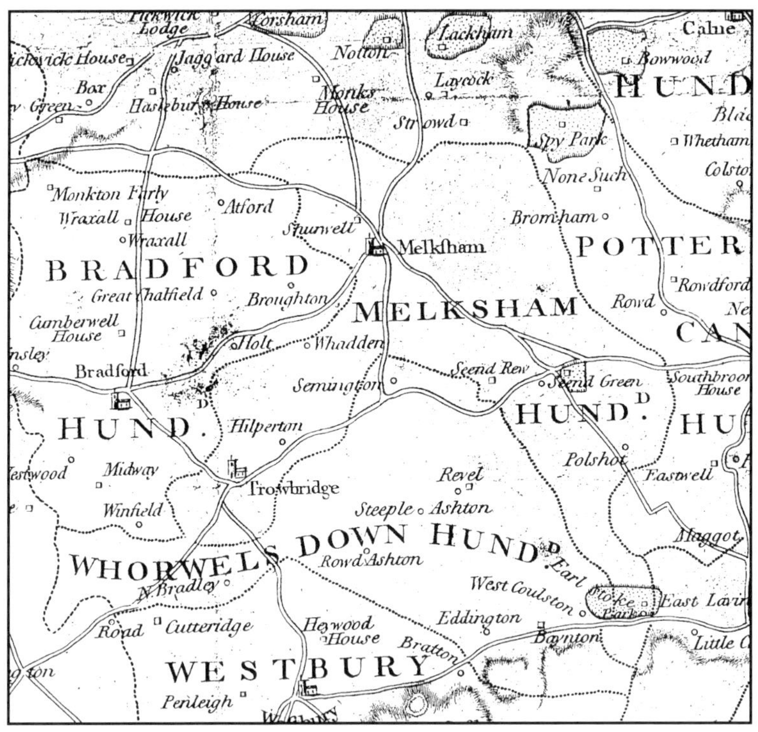

Tunnicliff, 1791. WRO.

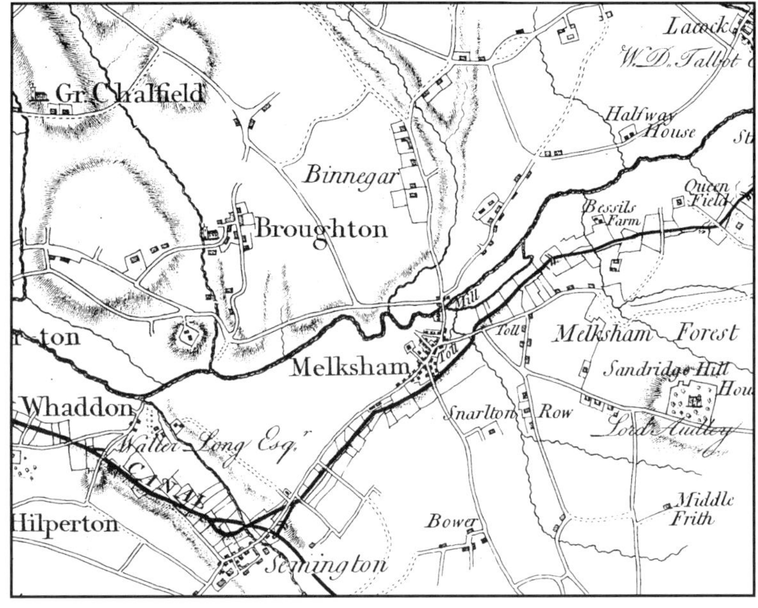

R & W Whitworth, 1793. WRO.

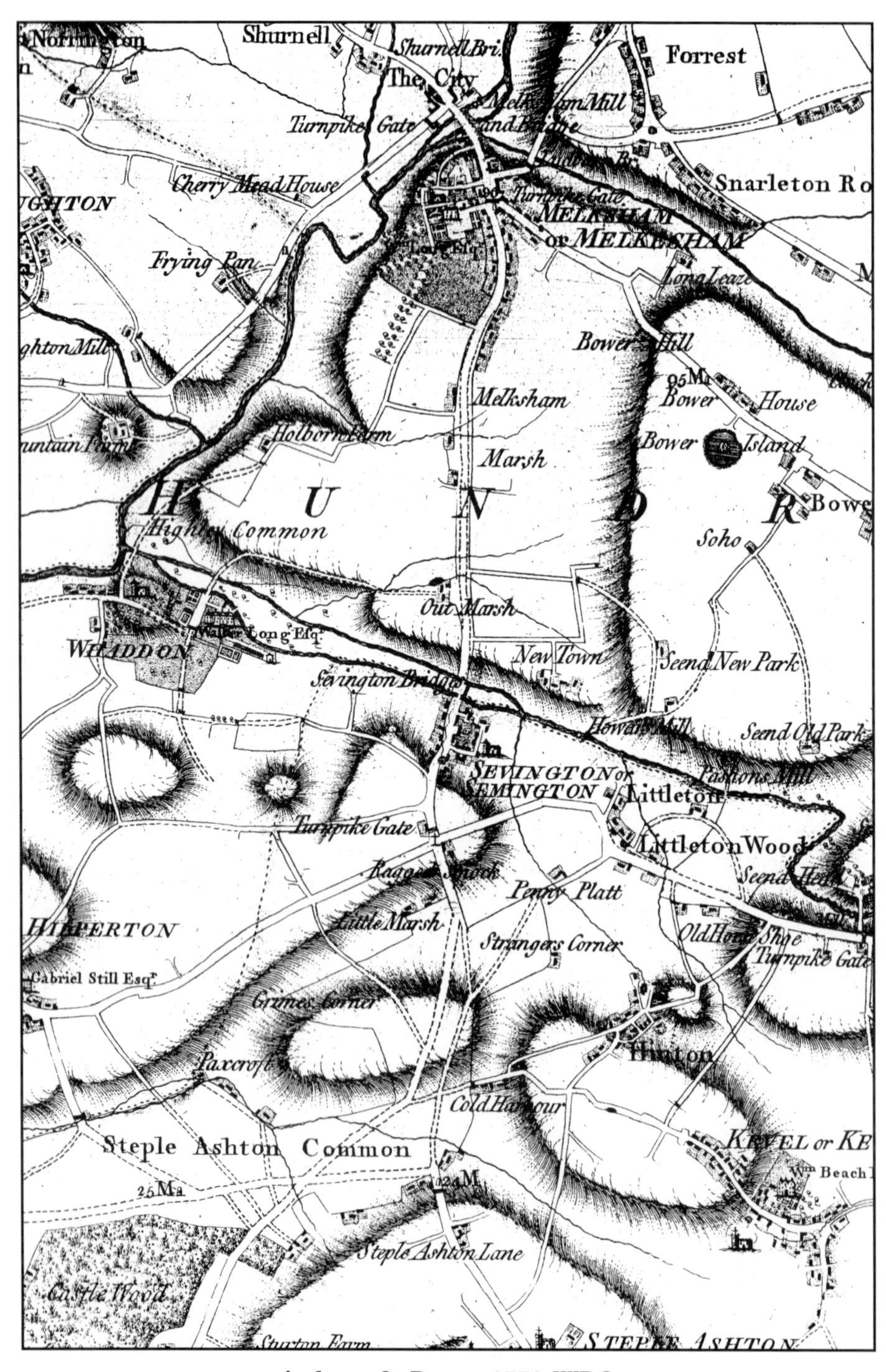

Andrews & Drury, 1773. WRO.

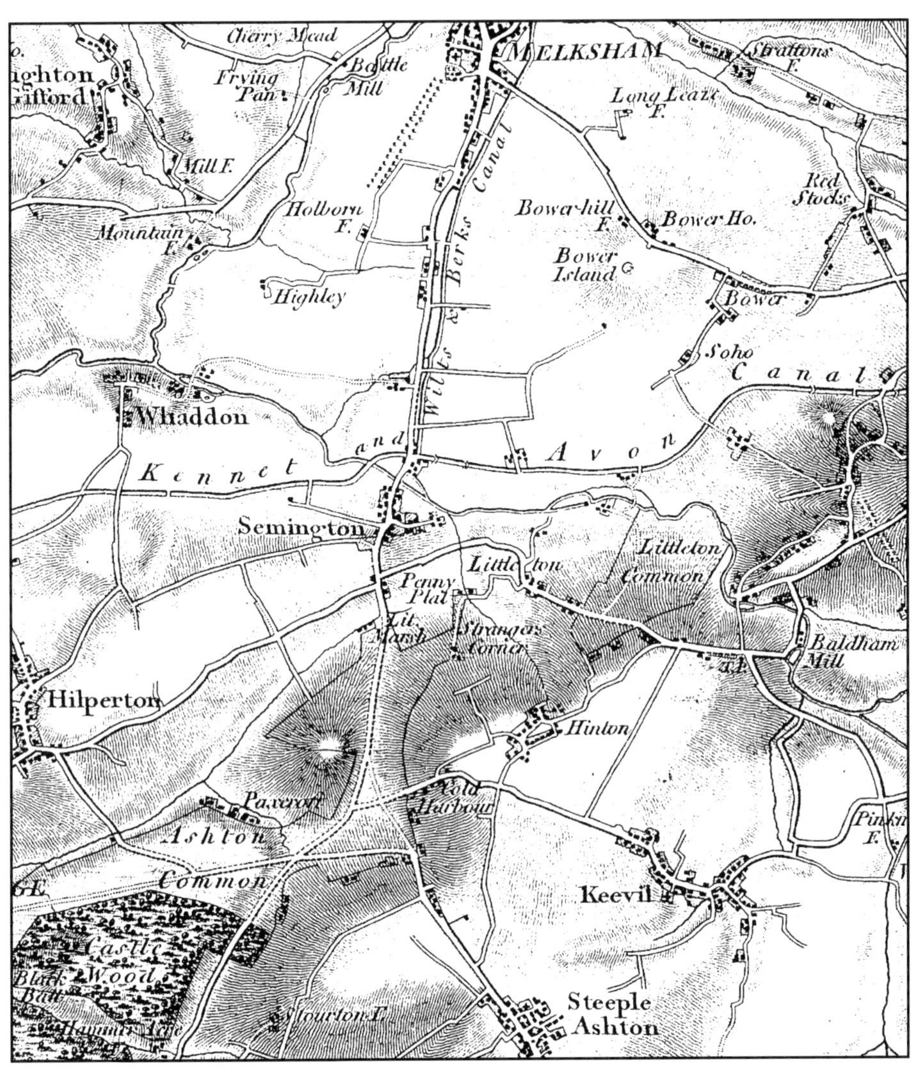

Ordnance Survey, 1817. WRO.

was not proceeded with. This map even shows individual buildings in Semington and makes a considerable advance in cartography, showing great detail, including some toll points, and the route of the W & B Canal and surroundings.

Also in 1793 Andrews and Drury moved mapping forward by showing roads of different widths according to their importance and also by accurate representation of bends and road junctions, even on minor roads.

We then move forward to 1817 and the first of the genuine Ordnance Survey maps, where the emphasis changed from depiction to extreme accuracy, based on surveying from a number of fixed stations. This map showed the new Kennet and Avon Canal. Later this system was refined further with a series of concrete blocks surmounted by an inverted concrete cone with a metal pin projecting from the top. These accurately located geographical points were known as triangulation stations and appear denoted on modern maps. By cross-referencing between the known stations even isolated buildings could be positioned with certainty.

In 1819 Greenwood added more detail like individual farms and footpaths (rights of way)

The 1837 Tithe Map shows fields and properties, each with a Tithing Number from which, using the Key below, individual owners, tenants and description of the property can be determined.

KEY TO 1837 TITHE MAP

NO.	OWNER	OCCUPIER	NAME/DESCRIPTION
79	Thomas Bruges	William Gulliver	Great Leasehold
81	William Matravers	Himself	House, Building Gdn & Orchard
82	Hester Bruges	Harriet Millard	House & Garden
83	W. Heald & Thos Bruges	William Gulliver	Home Orchard
84	James Bendy	Himself	House, Building & Garden
85	W. Heald & Thos Bruges	William Gulliver	Waggon & Horses & Premises
86	The Duke of Somerset	Richard Hawkins	House & Garden
87	William Matravers	Himself	Goodwards
88	Thomas Bruges	William Gulliver	Little Leasehold
89	Sarah Taylor Bruges	Thomas Vincent	House, Garden & Orchard
90	do	James Pocock	Patch
91	do	do	Home Ground
92	William Matravers	Himself	Limekiln

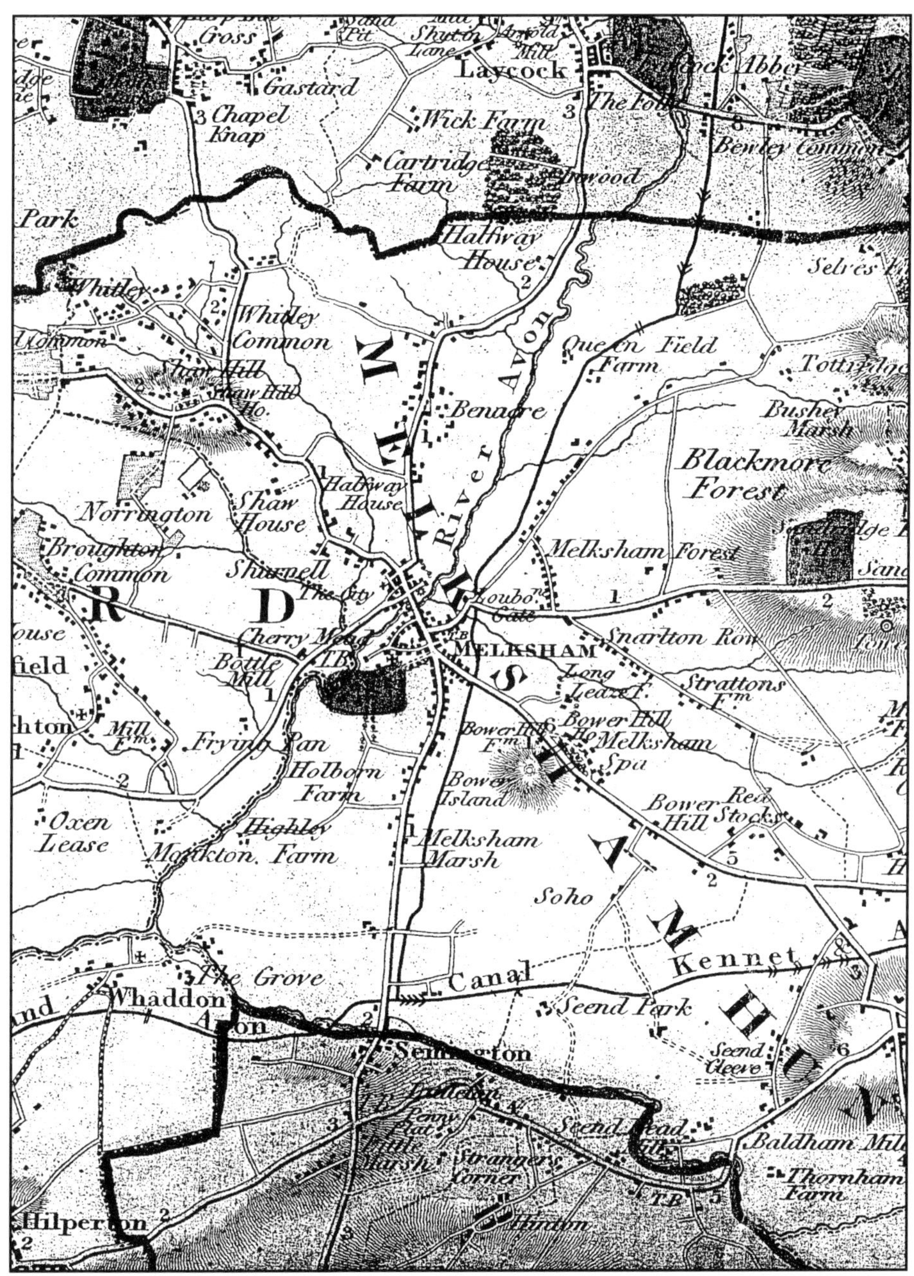

Greenwood, 1819. WRO.

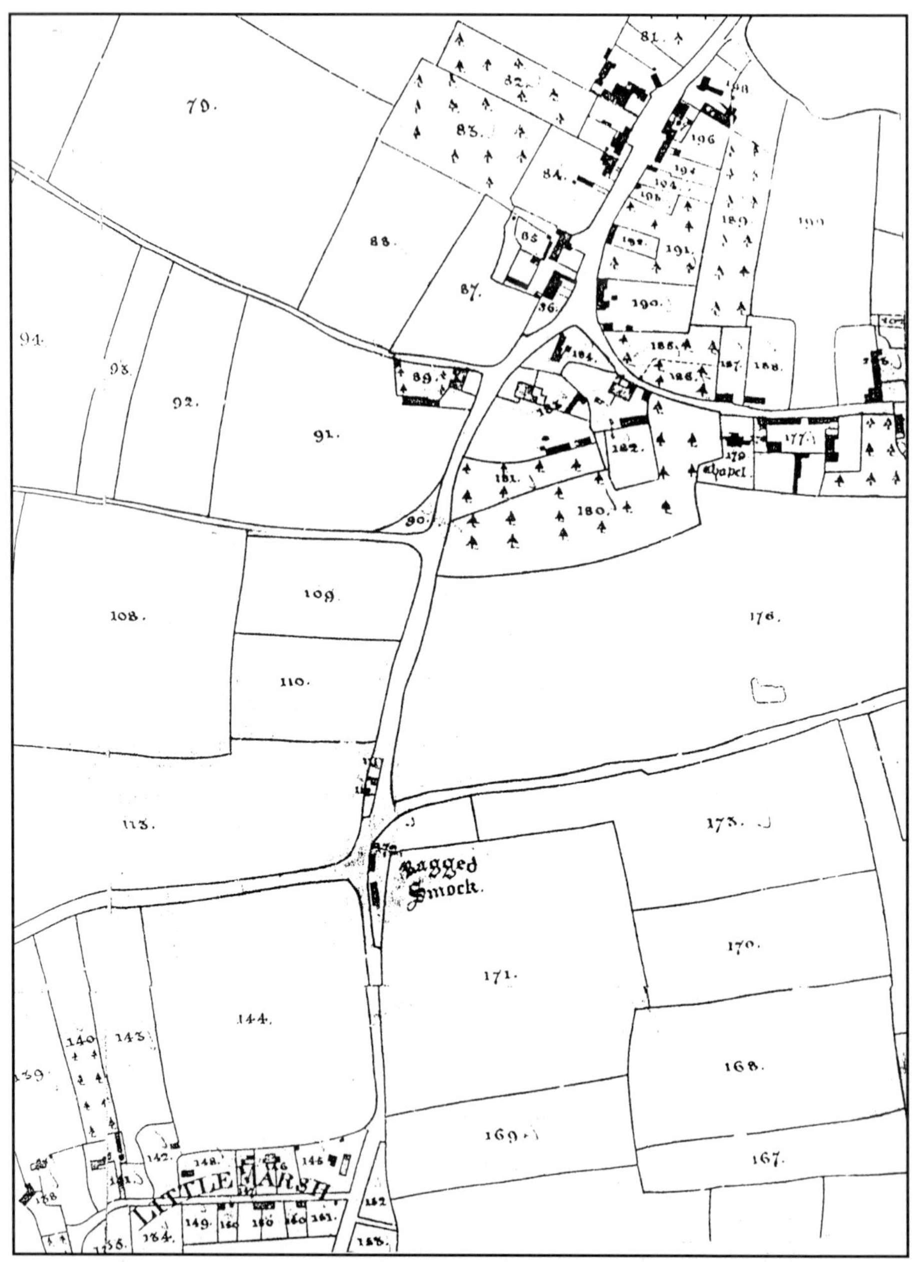

Tithe Map, 1837. WRO.

93	Semington Chapel Trustees	William Gulliver	Church Acres
94	All Souls College	Thomas Bruges	Six Acres
108	The Duke of Somerset	James Pocock	New Inclosure
109	W Heald & Thos Bruges	William Gulliver	Little Knap Ground
110	Sarah Taylor Bruges	James Pocock	Home Field
111	The Duke of Somerset	Himself	The Manor Pound
112	Turnpike Commissioners	William Gulliver	House & Garden
113	The Duke of Somerset	James Pocock	Horsley
134	James Chapman	Richard Hawkins	Little Marsh
135	The Duke of Somerset	Richard Hawkins	Little Marsh
138	do	do	House & Garden
139	do	do	Bartletts
140	W Heald & Thos. Bruges	George Wilshire	Orchard Close
141	do	do	House, Buildings & Garden
142	Thos Bruges &c.	Robert Bigwood	House & Garden
143	Walter Long	Joseph Ghey	Ballards Close
144	All Souls College	Thomas Bruges	Marsh Furling
145	James Pocock	John Loule	House & Garden
146	Thos Bruges &c	John Smart	House & Garden
147	do	Isaac Gulliver	House & Garden
148	William Gulliver	Susan Gulliver	House & Garden
149	David Sims	Himself	Garden
150	Roger Watts	Himself	House & Garden
162	Rev. Thos Gaisford	Joseph Ghey	Broad Croft
167	do	do	Long Croft
168	All Souls College	Thomas Bruges	Plow'd Hempshills
169	do	do	Hempshills
170	Rev.G. Chamberlain	Thomas Milsom	The Crofts
171	Walter Long	John Hayward	Ragged Smock Ground
172	The Duke of Somerset	William Gulliver	House, Garden & Orchard
173	Rev. G. Chamberlain	Thomas Milsom	The Crofts
176	The Duke of Somerset	William White	Home Ground
177	do	do (Church Farm)	House, Buildings, Gdn & Orchard
178	Semington Chapel Trustees	James May	House & Garden
179	do	Themselves	Chapel & Yard
180	All Souls College	Thomas Bruges	Hunts Close

181	The Duke of Somerset	Hester Bruges	Home Orchard
182	All Souls College	Thomas Bruges	House, Buildings & Garden
183	Hester Bruges	Herself	House, Buildings Gdn & Orchard
184	Thos & Wm Bruges	William Wiltshire	House, Buildings & Garden
185	Mary Curtis	William Wiltshire	Orchard
186	The Duke of Somerset	Mary Curtis	Orchard
187	do	James Pocock	House & Garden
188	George Taylor	Joseph Weeks	House & Garden
189	Mary Curtis	William Wiltshire	Lower Orchard
190	Walter Long	Robert Wiltshire	House, Buildings Gdn & Orchard
191	Sarah Taylor Bruges	James Pocock	Home Orchard
192	The Duke of Somerset	do	House & Garden
193	do	William Matravers	House & Garden
194	Thomas Sims	Himself	House & Garden
195	Sarah Taylor Bruges	Thomas Miller	House & Garden
196	William Matravers	Ann Mercer	House & Garden
197	do	Himself	House & Garden
198	Mary Curtis	Herself	House, Buildings Gdn & Orchard
199	The Duke of Somerset	William White	Hithertons
204	do	James Pocock	House, Buildings Gdn , Yard, &c. (Manor Farm)
205	do	do	Home Orchard
206	do	do	Home Orchard

The Ordnance Survey Map of 1901 depicts the railway track passing west to east just north of Outmarsh Farm, before there was a stop for Semington. The Ordnance Survey Map of 1924 shows the addition of Semington Halt (built in 1906).

The surveying system was, and is now, an ongoing process and resulted in periodic re-issuing of maps which eventually formed a complete lattice covering the British Isles and later some overseas countries.

The latest techniques used in cartography include aerial photography and satellite imaging.

Ancient sites are often covered by layers of soil or some form of overburden and hence not visible on the surface unless some recognisable earthworks project or depressions in some geometrical pattern contrast with the surroundings. Another indication of the presence of an ancient site which would not normally be noticed can be seen in “crop marks”. This form of recognition can only be seen when a growing crop has freshly broken through the surface. The presence a short distance underground of some material which is different from the surrounding soil causes the young crop to exhibit

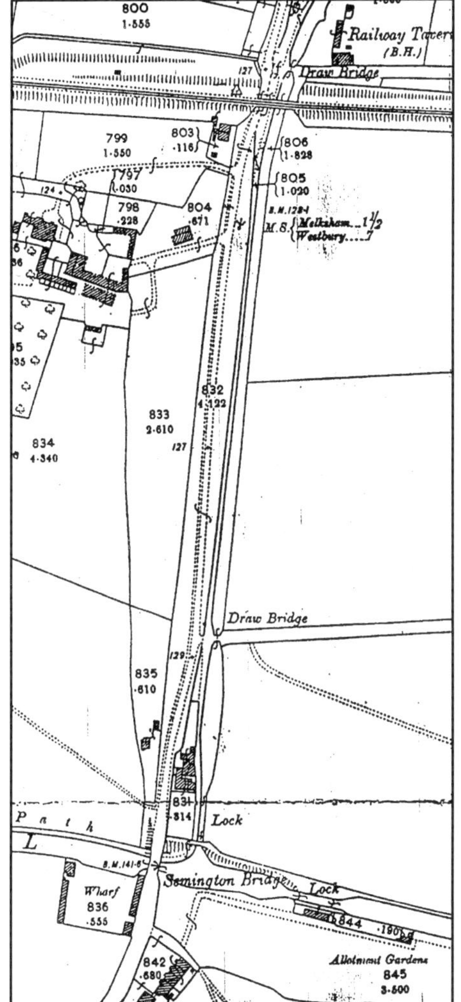

Ordnance Survey, 1901.WRO.

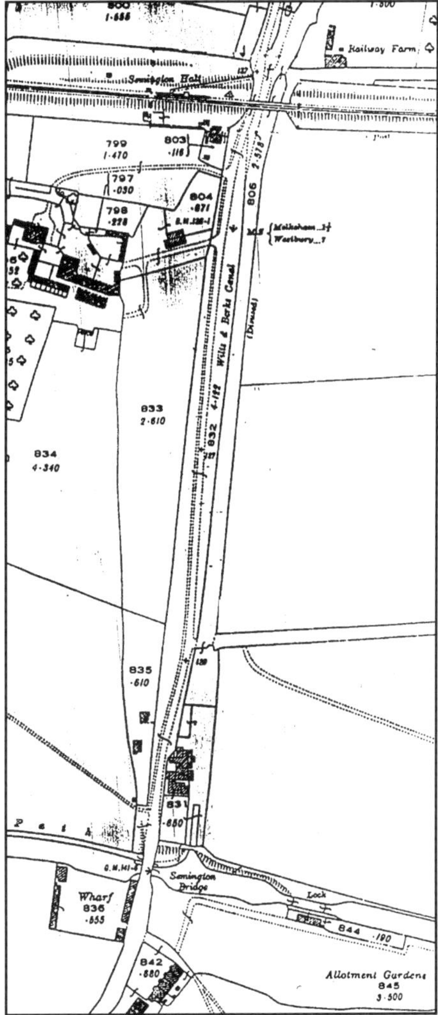

Ordnance Survey, 1924.WRO.

a slightly different growing pattern, usually visible as a small colour change above the submerged material.

Several sites in Semington have been documented by the Wiltshire County Council Sites and Monuments Record:

1. *At Bartletts Farm, Semington:* a buried Post-Medieval Settlement. Home of William Bartlett, A D 1624.

2. *Littlemarsh:* Small group of undated earthworks.

3. *Whaddon:* Flint instruments and waste flint.

4. *Whaddon:* Romano-British pottery fragments suggesting a villa nearby

5. *Semington:* Buried late Medieval settlement Semel(e)ton AD 1249

6. *Whaddon:* Settlement with Medieval origins. 13th and 14th century Pottery fragments, Iron dagger Settlement Wadone AD 1086

7. *Littleton Green Farm, Semington:* Earthworks of late Medieval settlement covering 34 hectares. Some pottery found.

8. *Littleton Mill Farm, Semington:* 1/2 hectare of undated earthworks.

An area of earthworks at Littleton (mainly in a field called Bar Crofts in the Tithe Award of 1838) was discovered by Roy Canham and Alison Borthwick during aerial photography in 1978. Further research by the Junior Section of the Wiltshire Archaeological and Natural History Society revealed some sherds of medieval pottery. In Volume 78 of the *Wiltshire Archaeological and Natural History Magazine* the aerial photograph is accompanied by an article by Mrs P. M. Slocombe, in which she points out that of the few other houses shown in Littleton on the Tithe Map the most notable is Littleton Wood Farm, which documentary evidence and subsequent examination by the Wiltshire Buildings Record has shown to be a substantial residence in the small Manor (or sub-manor) of Littleton, which area contains a water mill of medieval origin on a leat of the Semington Brook less than half a mile to the north-east of the earthworks.

Aerial view of earthworks at Littleton, 1978.. From Wiltshire Archaeological & Natural History Magazine, *no. 78, pp. 121-123. (Courtesy Roy Canham).*

Remains of Littleton Mill Wharf

Remains of Pump House (Courtesy Mrs J. Fry)

Remains of Rifle Range Butts. (Courtesy Mr P. Hamphries)

Chapter 5

EDUCATION

The first indication of any form of schooling in Semington can be found in a copy of part of the Will of Thomas Somner, late of Wellow, in the County of Somerset, which is with Semington's Chapelwardens' Accounts (now in Wiltshire Record Office) and dated 1699:[1]

> "...Also I doe give devise and bequeath one Rent Charge or Sume of Forty Shillings to be Yearly and every Year for ever issueing and payable out of all my Messuages Lands Tenements and Hereditaments situate lying and being in Steeple Ashton Littleton and Semington in the County of Wilts and to be paid and applied Yearly for the schooling of two Poor Boys of the Tything of Semington aforesaid to be Yearly nominated from time to time by the Overseers of the Poor of Semington aforesaid for the time being."

At the time of his death Thomas Somner owned, as well as other lands in Littleton, the fulling and grist mill, which was then called Passion's Mill (after a previous owner) and is now known as Littleton Mill.

Very occasionally over the following years Thomas Somner's Will is mentioned in the Chapelwardens' Accounts and children are nominated to be educated - six in 1771, including one girl. In 1775 two boys are selected "for Joan the Wife of Richd Drinkwater to instruct the said Boys". In 1849 four boys are sent "to the School of this Chapelry, free of charge". Other records show that by 1799 there was a Sunday school in Semington, paid for by subscription from a number of the more well-to-do members of the community. A note from Mr. Vaudrey, the Curate at that time, informs "the members of the Vestry that the present subscription [£3.5s.] is not sufficient to pay the wages of the Schoolmaster". Other papers show that Mr David Marks, the Schoolmaster, was paid £4.4s. a year from 1799 to 1803, after which his wife - "the widow Marks" - took over and continued to run the Sunday School until 1811. The actual registers still exist, from 1803 to 1810,[2]

Semington School pupils, 1914. (Courtesy Mr D. Barnett)

Semington School pupils, 1920. (Courtesy Mr D. Barnett)

listing each boy and girl and their attendances every Sunday throughout the year - their absences being shown by an "x". Reasons for the frequent absences are shown as "sheepkeeping", "cow keep", "bird keep", "no shoes", "no clothes" or "bad foot" and, once or twice against the name of a girl, "gone to service". There does not appear to have been an actual school building in the village at that time, so lessons may have taken place in the Chapel, although by 1839 Mr Thomas Bruges was being paid £3.3s. "for rent of the Schoolroom". The lists of subscribers towards the cost of the Sunday School run from 1799 to 1839, by which time there were 18 contributors, including the Duke of Somerset (who paid £2). The total came to £9.10s.6d., out of which £5 was paid to the teacher, James Sainsbury (who was also the Parish Clerk), £3.3s. for rent and 12/6d. to Mr. William Wilshire, for coals.

The 1851 Census Return for Semington, Littleton and Paxcroft names 44 children as "scholars" and one Schoolmistress, Elizabeth Wilshire. Whether Mrs Wilshire was teaching in Semington and whether there was a day school by that time is not recorded.

By the late 1840s and in accordance with various Acts of Parliament for the "endowment of Sites for Schools" plans were afoot for the building of a School. In January 1859 a document signed by the eight Trustees of "The Semington Chapel Charity Lands" granted a Deed of Gift of Land adjoining the Churchyard, numbered 178 on the Tithe Map, for the erection of a School "for the Education of Children or Adults or Children only of the Labouring, Manufacturing or other poorer Class... and as a Residence for the Teacher or Teachers of the said School... which said School shall always be in Union with and conducted upon the Principles and in furtherance of the Established Church".[3] It is believed that the building then on the site, which was demolished to make way for the school, had been known as "Church House" and had been at one time the residence of the Curate-in-Charge of Semington, before the Parsonage was built.

The school was erected in 1859 and was in use until 1968, when the new school in Pound Lane was built.

National School, built 1859

Old School now private house

The old building still exists, although it is now a private house. Some idea of what it was like to be a pupil in the school in the 1930s will be found in the chapter on "Reminiscences".

By the 1861 Census there were 56 "scholars" and one 16 year old boy (George Gaisford) was recorded as a "pupil teacher". There were also two "Governesses", one living at Semington House, with Mr and Mrs Thomas Bruges, and one at Brook Cottage, living with Mr and Mrs Bird, but there is no mention of a "Schoolmistress", so perhaps whoever was in charge of the school was living elsewhere. By 1871 another boy (George Gulliver) had been appointed "Pupil Teacher" and there was a Schoolmistress (Ruth Miles) living on her own - possibly at the School.

Apart from the Sunday School registers mentioned earlier no school records have been found before 1875, when Semington School Log Book begins on 4th January, as the school re-opened after the Christmas vacation and Alice Honniball commenced her duties as Mistress.[4] When the school begins again, after the harvest vacation in August, Mary Guley has become the Mistress, and comments: "The children appear to have been neglected as they did not seem to understand anything about 'Order'."

Mary Guley obviously tried hard to instil some discipline, but apparently with little effect. In March 1876 she cautioned the children "about using filthy language and writing it about in different places on walls", but eventually the rough behaviour and the lack of attendance seems to have been too much for her and she resigned in December 1876. On 15th January 1877 Harriet Meuton commenced duties as Mistress, but resigned on account of illness on the 29th of the same month, to be succeeded by Agnes R. Taylor on the 30th. Agnes managed to stay the course until December 1878, when she resigned on account of ill-health. She was replaced by Betty Hutchings in January 1879, but when the school re-opened after the harvest vacation in September 1882, the Mistress was Emily Langley. She resigned five years later, on 30th September, 1887 and was replaced by James Osborne as Master (pro-tem) until December 1887. In January 1888 the school re-opened with Frances Rabbitts assuming duties as Mistress. According to the 1891 Census she was living in a four-roomed cottage with her 12 year old sister, Mabel. Francis resigned in August 1893, being replaced temporarily by Margaret Lewis, from September to December. She was followed by Frances Osmon, who managed five years, from 1893 to July 1898. Alice Munday then took over, from September 1898 to February 1907, with F. M. Hancock as her assistant. Miss Munday was replaced by Edith Rees, from 1907 to 1908, followed by Edith Stocker until 1909, when Millicent Dowse became Head Teacher. In 35 years there had been fifteen different teachers managing the school.

Semington School pupils, 1930. (Courtesy Mr D. Barnett)

Anyone anxious to know what the weather in Semington was like a hundred years ago need look no further than Semington School Log Book. From 1879 to 1920 scarcely a year went by without reference to heavy snow, flooding, gales and storms during the winter months and at other times, all combining to prevent the children from getting to school, plus the added impediment of whooping cough, chicken pox., scarletina, measles, coughs and colds and mumps. The sparse attendance appears to have given the School Attendance Officer some concern, but despite the fact that the school was closed in August to enable the children to take part in the harvesting, they were often called away at other times for haymaking, pea, potato or fruit picking - a reminder that this was a farming community and the first concern of everyone living there was with the land. There were two occasions - noted for their rarity - when the number on the school books equalled the number of children present.

Half holidays were also allowed for "Gooding" on St Thomas's Day (21st December) when the children went about knocking on doors and wishing the residents well, in return for alms of some kind. Then there was the Annual Treat given by the Vicar at Steeple Ashton, or Lady Long at Rood Ashton, a half day off for Semington Annual Fair, later to be called St. George's Fete, which took place in late April or early May, and in June, 1887, two days off to celebrate Queen Victoria's Jubilee, to be followed the next year with a special Tea, provided from the proceeds remaining from the previous year's festivities.

Because it was a Church school, the children were visited on a regular basis by both the Vicar of Steeple Ashton and the Curate in Charge of Semington, who gave lessons in Religious Knowledge and generally kept an eye on the school. Various ladies of the village (including the Curates' wives and daughters) took an interest and occasionally gave lessons in Needlework or Knitting, or Scripture.

It must be remembered that before the Free Education Act of 1891 the parents paid for their children's education and on one occasion two pupils were sent home because they arrived without their fees.

Some mention must be made of the outside world: the death of King Edward VII was recorded, as was the Accession of George V in May 1910. Empire Day was regularly celebrated from 1912, and on 2nd May 1912 a postal order and stamps to the value of 7s.3d. was sent to the *Daily Mail* towards the *Titanic* Disaster Fund.

No mention was made of the start of the Great War, but in July 1915 the children collected 5s.10d. for the French Relief Fund and sang the Marseillaise. In 1916 some 5,000 soldiers passed through the village en route for Trowbridge, so the children were allowed to watch them. In November 1917 children and teachers lined up in the centre of the village, waving flags and cheering, as King George V and Queen Mary passed through Semington on the way from Trowbridge to Melksham on their tour of the West of England. 18 motor cars were counted in their entourage.

In September and October 1918 the children went blackberrying "for the Army and Navy" under a special scheme, and were given half-holidays for that purpose. Altogether they picked nearly 250 lbs, for which they were paid.

News of the Armistice was received on 11th November and the children marched through the village at the close of the morning session with "musical" instruments and carrying flags. The National Anthem was sung and they were then dismissed for the afternoon.

Form 4a.

DIOCESE OF SALISBURY. Deanery of Bradford

Diocesan Inspection of Schools.

Inspector's Report of Semington School ______ Department

Inspected 29th June 1939

I was very pleased with the good work of this school.
The lessons in both classes were given concisely & clearly, & good use was made of the subjects selected.
In response to questions the children shewed a good understanding of their work.

Signed [illegible]

Diocesan Inspector.

This Report should be entered in the Log Book.

Inspection Certificate, 1939. (Courtesy Mrs S Gilbert)

FROM MRS E. GRACE BURBIDGE:

It was wartime when I was appointed as Head Teacher of St George's School, Church Street, Semington, in September 1942.

The east end of the Church and the churchyard wall was the boundary on one side. The cowshed against the cloakroom wall and the farmyard was on the opposite side. The toilets and the large heap of coke were the south side. There was a corrugated iron fence along the middle of the playground to separate the girls from the boys. I asked for this to be removed.

Due to the war, money and materials were in short supply. Paper was precious and we saved used envelopes, etc. The Infant classroom on the north side was for the 5 - 7+s and the other, larger, classroom was for the 7 - 14s.

Each day started with Assembly for the whole school and included an Act of Worship. On one morning each week Canon Yerburgh and later Canon Youngman took this, followed by a lesson with the 7 - 14s. The Salisbury Diocesan Religious Syllabus was used throughout the year for the whole school. On Special Days the school went into the Church for a Service, for which I played the organ, (I had been taught to play by a blind man who was a church organist when I was at primary school, and since then have loved the Anglican Church music particularly).

School outing to Cheddar and Weston, 1946. (Courtesy Mr D. Barnett)

After Assembly we kept to our own classrooms for the rest of the day. Mornings for everyone consisted of English, Reading and Mathematics, all of which was done in groups. English included Spelling, taught chiefly phonetically, and Grammar. Maths included mental and practical work. The last lesson of each day was Literature, usually with the whole class.

Afternoons were spent on History, Geography, Nature Study, Art, Handwork and Music. Nature Study included studying flora and fauna in the environment, and we walked in the fields and lanes and the brookside and canalside. We made a garden near the yew tree in the S.E. corner of the rear of the churchyard, to which we had access through a small gate from the playground. We often saw slowworms emerging from the old, dilapidated tombs on which they basked in the sun.

When the Church was redecorated, the organ was taken to pieces to be cleaned and renovated. The workmen showed us their work as they progressed. On the last day we all surveyed their handiwork. The foreman told us it was a pity the metalwork was not decorated with gold leaf but the money did not run to that. So on the spur of the moment I pledged the school to pay for it to be done. We raised the money in numerous ways, with much interest and effort by the children.

We also raised the money for electricity to be installed in the school. It was in the adjoining cowsheds, but we had oil lamps. Both classrooms were heated by coke Tortoiseshell stoves which had to be lighted at the beginning of each week, using coal from the coal shed. Mr. and Mrs. Humphries carried out this unenviable task of lighting and cleaning them and carrying the coke from the playground. They also cleaned the building and were general caretakers. When they retired Mr and Mrs Wiscombe continued the work. They cleared paths in the snow during the winter, when the taps in the cloakroom froze.

The part of the classroom furthest from the stove was chilly, so sometimes an Aladdin oil stove at that end had to be used. During the summer, when the stoves were not lighted, the rooms had a chilly feel, but in a heatwave it was refreshingly cool. To boil a kettle we then used a Beatrice oil stove. One morning this went up in flames and I had to carry it through the cloakroom into the playground.

The big boys used to collect milk each morning from Manor Farm for those who wanted it. They used a can and we had to serve it around. Later it was delivered in bottles by Sheate's Dairy in Melksham.

Semington School pupils, 1959, with Mrs Robinson – in light-colouered dress. (Courtesy Mr D. Barnett)

In bad weather we did limited stretching exercises between the desks. Otherwise we did PE and games in the playground. When there was snow I allowed snowballing, providing they did not throw in the direction of the windows. No one ever took advantage and I used to hear the older children ensuring that the younger ones did not break the rule. We never suffered from vandalism. Many of the children lived in or near Church Street.

Numbers increased with children from the RAF camp and Berryfield and we became overcrowded. So the schoolroom in the Methodist Chapel at the end of Church Street was hired, first of all for mornings only, and later for longer periods. We engaged part-time staff to teach the 7 - 9s there, first of all Mrs Cuff and later Mrs Godfrey. They trekked there after Assembly.

Hot meals could then be ordered from County Hall for those who wanted them. They were delivered in metal containers. Mrs. Wiscombe was appointed dinner lady and Mrs. Nash playground supervisor for the lunch hour. After a while County Hall hired the Village Hall part-time for lunch there. We had to escort the children across the busy road and I acted as "lollipop lady".

When we moved to the new school Mrs Pearce was appointed cook and Mrs Hervin and Mrs Wiscombe helpers. We had excellent cooked food.

As soon as it could be arranged, on one afternoon a week the children went to Bradford on Avon for swimming lessons. The flat roof leaked

New school under construction, 1967. (Courtesy Mrs P. Mortimer)

constantly during wet weather. But the warmth and sunshine through the windows was bliss, as was the space.

Many of my ex-pupils are OAPs so I do not recognise them. I visualise them as pupils and can remember their strengths and difficulties. I enjoy their letters, cards and photographs, rejoice in their successes and pray for help in their misfortunes and difficulties. Some have pre-deceased me; sadly, two little girls when in our Infant class. But I am sustained by my Christian faith and belief that we shall all meet again in a better place.'

POSTSCRIPT

In 1968, when the new school in Pound Lane was being built, the then vicar of Steeple Ashton, the Reverend A. R. Moore, noticed a request, in a circular from the United Society for the Propagation of the Gospel, from the Reverend Canon James Mudhoo, of St Thomas Rectory, Beau Bassin, Mauritius, for a bell for his Church. Knowing that the old school in Semington was for sale, and that the bell which had called the children to school for over a hundred years would be surplus to requirements, the Reverend Moore contacted the Reverend Mudhoo, via the USPD, offering him Semington's school bell. for his Church.. The Reverend Mudhoo replied in November 1968, thanking the Reverend Moore warmly for his "beau geste" and accepting the offer. The problem then was how to get the bell to Mauritius.

Fortunately, there was living at that time in Steeple Ashton Commander W. Lock, of the Royal Navy. Somehow or other he managed to arrange for the bell (which by that time had been taken down, cleaned and fixed with a new clapper) to be transported by the Royal Navy, via the RFA *Bacchus*, from Tilbury to Mauritius, it would appear entirely free of charge. The bell arrived:

there was a handing over ceremony - photographs were taken, which were sent back to the Revd. Moore, and the local newspapers in both areas ran the story.

School bell in Mauritius. (Courtesy Mr D. Burbidge).

SEMINGTON St. GEORGE'S SCHOOL IN THE PRESENT DAY

by Suzanne Gilbert, Head Teacher from 1988 to the present.

'I feel privileged as the current headmistress of St. George's School to be contributing to this research. As a start I scanned the current logbook, which is still in school. I will do as I should according to the 'thirty year rule' and avoid direct quotes, but draw some conclusions from the detailed reports of the head teachers, who have led the school since the retirement of Mrs Burbidge.

I expected to see nothing but differences from the present day, but to my surprise found a number of similarities in many areas, as well as many changes.

All the reports about the maintenance of the 'new' school bear a remarkable similarity to the present day. The roof still leaks, the drains get blocked and the paint still peels. The field was open for village use at weekends, but sadly too much damage was caused to the school and it is now restricted to supervised use. But that school field is still host to a range of social activities provided by the Friends of St. George's, to sports afternoons and inter school football matches. Yes, we still both win and lose them, but the participating children continue to learn about teamwork and trying their best.

We still take part in many activities, which involve the whole village. I am proud of the country dancing and exhibitions of work the pupils provide for the annual Church Fete. We had a splendid time joining in the 50 Year celebrations of V.E. Day and the events to mark the Millennium.

The day-to-day life of the school is little different, with teachers still going on training courses to keep up with new developments, and inspectors checking the work of the children to see all is well. What a pity they are no longer allowed to grant the children a half-day holiday for doing good work! Our latest inspection last year found much to commend, but realistically recognised the problems we have with space and delivering the full I.C.T. curriculum. We still find time to go on trips to many different places and then find from looking in the logbook that it has all been done before. Thank goodness for the pantomime and the Bristol Zoo, which our children have visited over many decades.

The biggest changes that have beset St. George's in recent years have been in the increased central control of the content and teaching style of the curriculum and the delegation of finances to the school.

When I came here some fourteen years ago it was generally up to the school to decide what should be taught to the children. We followed some County guidelines and the standard school textbooks that everyone used. We put the child at the centre of the curriculum and planned the work around their individual and group needs. We used some tests to evaluate progress and were pleased to see the pupils achieve knowledge and skills to benefit them both in their academic and 'real' life. Over the last ten years we have seen the development of a standardised national curriculum, which lays out the content of all subjects, and more latterly the Literacy and Numeracy initiatives that dictate how this content should be taught. The standards that 'normal' children are expected to achieve in English and Maths are tied to national targets, which at present are adjusted upwards each year, although there are now some voices of reason at national level, recognising the impossibility of this. It has been some ten years of constant change with little chance for teachers or pupils to catch their breath. I am happy to celebrate all the good things that have come out of these changes, but I hope that soon a little more autonomy will be returned to the schools themselves.

Pupils and staff, 2002.

The centralisation of the curriculum has been matched by a shift in delegation of finances. In April 1988 the governors and myself were responsible for a budget of some three thousand pounds. For the last ten years most of a school's money has been given directly to the school, which at the financial year end each April has meant dealing with around one hundred and twentyfive thousand pounds, plus a host of grants, whose expenditure is strictly controlled. I used to have a twelve-column account book for monitoring the budget. Now there is a computer program, a school administrative officer and termly support from an accounting technician. The governors have to decide exactly how to spend this money, whilst the role of the education authority has been much reduced and handed to these hard-working volunteers. Their latest challenge has been to cope with a reduced budget, as there are less children in the village, but
still those here need the fabric of the building maintained, the same range of equipment, the teachers, helpers and dinner staff, who give so much. We still have a number of children who come to the school from Berryfields and Melksham and there are plans to build no less than ninety-eight new houses at the edge of the village.

So my concluding thoughts turn to the future in the hope that the school will continue to go from strength to strength. We look forward this year to taking our part in the Queen's Jubilee just as pupils did twentyfive years

New School. (Courtesy Mrs S. Gilbert).

ago. We have delightful pupils, who are so well behaved and hardworking, who go on to great success at secondary school and university. I have ex-pupils involved in a range of professions and, yes, even some have become teachers in their turn!'

References

1 Semington Chapelwardes' Accounts. WRO 714/8.
2 Semington Sunday School Records. WRO 714/42.
3 Semington Chapel Charity Lands. WRO 714/26.
4 Semington C of E primary School Log Book. WRO F8/500 239/1/1.

Former Bell Inn

Somerset Arms

Chapter 6

PUBLIC HOUSES, COACHING, TOLLROADS

PUBLIC HOUSES

Semington has over the years boasted four public houses, but not necessarily at the same time. This at first may seem excessive for what was a small village, but when one considers other similar villages with passing coaching and canal routes the number is not unusual.

The first evidence of any form of hostelry comes from the Will of William Stokes, of Semington, Yeoman, dated 1710, in which among many other bequests, he leaves his two daughters his "leasehold house and close in Semington in possession of John Phillips known as the sign of the Bell".[1] Further reference to "The Bell" in the 18th century is found in the archives of the Duke of Somerset , some of whose records of "Courts Baron" (which deal mainly with the transfer of property through inheritance or other means) still survive. One, dated 1758, refers to "the said premises now called or known by the name or the Sign of the Bell, formerly the Ragged Smock".[2]

An Indenture dated 1891 regarding the transfer from a private owner to Frome United Brewery "of a dwelling house now used as and licensed for a beerhouse and known as the Bell Inn" refers back to an earlier transfer of occupancy dated 1738.

Reference to the Census Returns shows that the first mention of "the Bell beerhouse" is in 1871, when Job Miles is in residence as "Farmer/Beer Retailer". Job Miles is first mentioned in the Census in 1841, when his occupation is given as "Farmer". In 1861 he is recorded as Inn Keeper and Farmer of 25 acres at "The Jolly Butcher". By 1881 William Messiter is the Innkeeper at The Bell, with Job Miles living with him as "retired Innkeeper". The Bell continued as a public house, situated opposite The Somerset Arms in the High Street, until it was closed in 1964. It is now a private house.

Another document, dated 1744/5, is signed by three "Parrishoners", testifying to the Justices of the Peace that in their opinion the "Dwelling House of Matthew Bruges in Semington was conveniently situated for a Victualling House, that he was of good reputation and that the same House was well Accommodated for Entertainment of Travellers".[3] This could well have been The Somerset Arms, which is believed to date from the 18th century. It is the only public house remaining in Semington, obviously named because the Duke of Somerset at one time owned most of the land upon which the village was built. It was and is a coaching inn, with sufficient outbuildings and accommodation to suggest that it was something more than a casual coaching halt. It is recorded in the Census Returns from 1851, the landlord at that time being "Innkeeper and Farmer of 67 acres". The landlords remained farmers as well as brewers or victuallers, up until 1901, when the landlord's occupation is given as "Publican and Pig Dealer".

The third inn was the Waggon and Horses which was on the site now occupied by the Village Hall. Other than knowing its position, as recorded in the 1837 Tithe Map, and that the Board of Guardians of the Workhouse used to hold their Board Meetings there before Melksham Union Workhouse[4] was built, the only other information found to date is that the licensee at one time was a Mr Gulliver, who also appeared to hold the post of Tollkeeper at the house near the crossroads.

The most intriguing of these hostelries was named The Ragged Smock. The Andrews & Drury Map dated 1773 prints the words "Ragged Smock" just south of the crossroads which then ran from Melksham to Little Marsh in one direction and from Hilperton to Littleton in the other. An early, unofficial census, probably taken by one of the Vicars of Steeple Ashton, dated 1801, shows that there were over a dozen people living at The Ragged Smock and in 1813 a similar list shows two houses containing 5 people. On the 1837 Tithe Map there is a reference to "Ragged Smock" just where the Andrews & Drury map had placed it 64 years before. What is mystifying is why not just one but several "Courts Baron" during the 18th century refer to "The Bell", formerly called "The Ragged Smock". Were there perhaps two pubs called "The Bell", or did the one establishment move from the crossroads down to the middle of the High Street, and if so, when?

The coaching route changed in the middle of the 19th century, so instead of stopping at the crossroads on the way from Devizes to Trowbridge the coaches came into the village and stopped at either the Waggon and Horses or the Somerset Arms on the way to Melksham, thus making an inn at the crossroads no longer necessary.

COACHING

The first coaches were introduced in this country from the Continent in the 16th century.

It was only about 1750 that road conditions improved to the extent that the stagecoach could succeed as a means of transport, considerably faster than the slow and heavy 'stage-waggon'. A typical journey time was London to Bath in 17 hours (the state of earlier roads caused journeys to be restricted to 30-40 miles per day).

Bath Mail taking up mail bags, late 18th century.

A stage coach usually held six, but occasionally eight people. It was a heavy vehicle, built strongly to withstand the excessive jolting caused by the bad roads. The body, which was covered with stout leather nailed to the frame with broad-headed nails, was slung by massive leather braces from upright posts springing from the axletrees of the front and rear wheels. When the coach was in motion, the body swung from side to side, and lurched and shook as well when the wheels met a more than usually uneven patch of road. Only the hardiest travellers were not afflicted with nausea, and many were obliged to take to their beds for a day or two after a journey. Even so the number of potential passengers was often greater than the number of available seats, and it was advisable to book in advance and to stay overnight at the inn in order to board the coach in the morning. The stagecoach system was based on changing horses about every 10 miles. The cost of travel was high: inside passengers were charged 5 pence or more per mile, outside passengers 2 pence or 3 pence per mile.

Bath Mail Coach halfpenny

The East/West London to Bath via Chippenham journey attracted many travellers as a more direct route (now represented by the A4 road). After 1750 the turnpiking of the parallel route through Devizes and Melksham opened up an easier road which became a popular alternative to the Chippenham route in the busiest years of the coaching era. Dishonest turnpike gatekeepers were all too common. The isolated position of the gates and the impossibility of maintaining a full-time check on the tolls, which had, or ought to have been collected, unfortunately encouraged fiddling and "private arrangements" with travellers.

In 1784 the first mail coach became operational, taking over from the postal service started in the 17th century, by which letters were carried along the principal highways by riders who changed horses at regular 'posts'. Bath and Bristol were connected to West Wiltshire by a network of local services (not touching Devizes, Warminster and Salisbury).

In 1828 there were 23 coaches daily from London to Bath, with one in the morning and one in the afternoon travelling via Devizes.

In 1795 the Devizes - Trowbridge coach ran 3 times per week, via Seend and Semington (Ragged Smock). In 1822 the service had increased to 9 per week. In 1830 this was reduced to 4 per week. By 1839 it had increased again

London and Bath steam carriage

to 18 plus a Melksham to Westbury via Semington service at 12 per week. In 1842 some obvious re-routing had taken place. The Devizes - Trowbridge and the Melksham - Westbury coaches now ran via Melksham and Semington at a rate of 24 coaches per week. By 1848 the service had disappeared.

LOCAL COACHES

Various coaches also ran on what could be described as a market/manufacturing town-connecting network and because no timetables have been traced it is assumed they ran on an "as required" basis, i.e., leaving when sufficient passengers had boarded the coach. This system would also account for many coaching inns being "waiting places" for the arrival of a coach.

The arrival of the Railway in Wiltshire by the early 1840s had an impact on the stagecoach operation. At first the coaches ran in reduced numbers and the routes were adjusted so that a service could be maintained but gradually thereafter the stagecoach service declined and finally was discontinued. The ending of the stagecoach system of travel also caused a considerable industrial downturn because Wiltshire alone supplied many hundreds of horses just to keep the inter-county and across county stagecoach transport system operational. As a final ignominy some of the smaller stagecoaches became used as transport to and from railway stations.

TOLL ROADS

Over the centuries there have been many pieces of legislation governing the state of the roads in England. At first the lords of the manor were responsible for the upkeep of the King's Highway, then in 1555 the Highway Act transferred the responsibility for the roads to the parishes, which meant that most parishioners were liable to give so many days a year of their own labour for the maintenance of the roads. By the eighteenth century the General Turnpike Act of 1772 enabled trusts to be established which had the right to collect a toll in exchange for maintaining a road ("turnpike" because a pike was placed across the road to act as a barrier until the traveller paid up).

There were a number of toll roads in Wiltshire: these were in general the connecting routes between towns. When the ground was soft and wet, great ruts would be cut into the earth road by the iron-hooped wooden wheels of horse-drawn coaches and heavy wagons. and it was necessary for the roadside ditches to be cleared in order to drain as much water away as possible.

To collect the toll money there would be a toll-keeper who normally lived in a toll house built beside the road at the toll point. One such house is recorded on the Andrews & Drury Map of 1773 at Semington, close to the Trowbridge to Devizes road, where the road to Melksham branches off. A second Turnpike Gate is shown just beyond Semington Parish Eastern Boundary on the Trowbridge -Devizes road at the Keevil road junction and yet a third is shown at Melksham across both the Semington-Melksham and the Melksham-Devizes roads. A fourth gate is shown on the Devizes-Holt road. The inference to be drawn from this number of toll points and their positioning is that there were enough well-used and well-defined coach routes in the area to justify the employment of the number of toll-keepers involved and the sum of money that could be collected.

Old main road and toll house.

References

1 *Wiltshire Notes & Queries* Vol. VI pp. 7 & 8

2 WRO 1332/17

3 WRO 714/47

4 Minutes of the Board of Guardians for Melksham Union Workhouse WRO H110/1/18

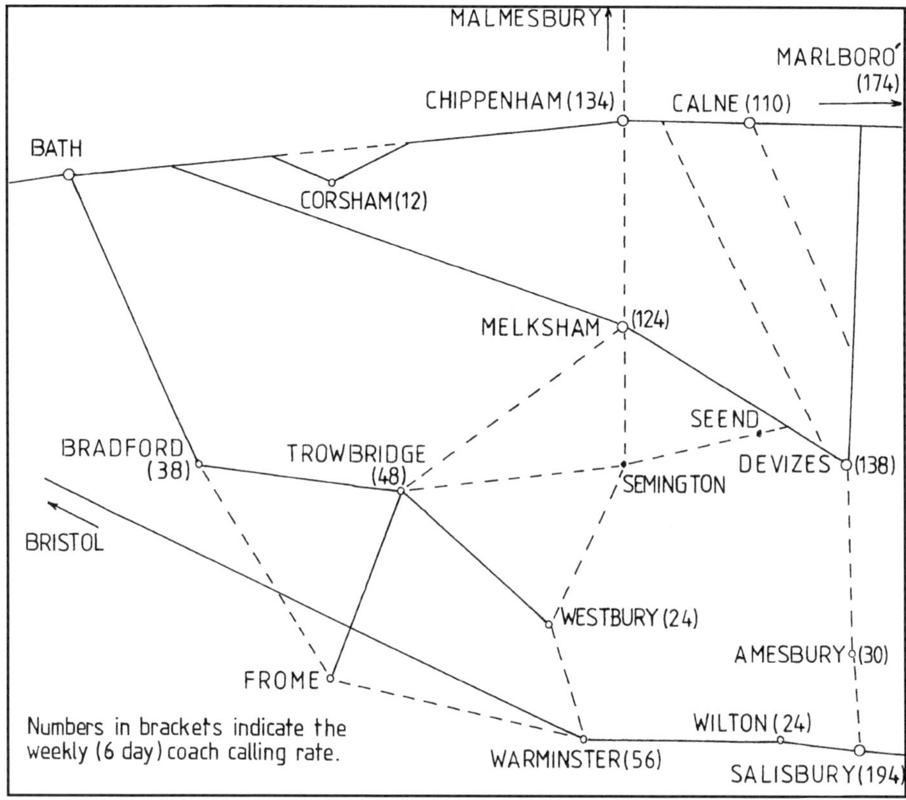

Coaching routes, 1795-1842 (after J. Copeland). The routes denoted by dotted lines only operated for part of this period. Some of these routes also had "fly" coaches (limited number of stops therefore quicker end to end journey times).

Outmarsh Farm

Wharf Cottage

Chapter 7

LISTED BUILDINGS

(Historic Structures listed by
Wiltshire Buildings Record)

Some of these buildings are listed under various parishes, because of Parish boundary changes which occurred from time to time, caused mainly by population movement

PARISH LISTED UNDER	BUILDING AND COMMENTS
Melksham Without (Semington sometime)	Outmarsh Farmhouse, Semington Road, Circa early C18 to Early C19. C19 addition (page 94)
Melksham Without	No. 541 Semington Road. Old Railway Farmhouse and the Sidings, previously the Railway Tavern. Included for interest only. Shown on railway map in Chapter 10
Melksham Without (now Semington)	Wharf Cottage. Canal Bridge, off Semington Road C18 with C20 extension (page 94)
Semington and Melksham Without	Semington Aqueduct. Off Semington Road Late C18-early C19 (page 98)
Semington	Manor Farmhouse, Church Street. Probably late 1500s. Altered C17 and C19 (page 107)
Semington	Granary at Manor Farm, Church Street (page 106) Datestone CP/1711. Flemish bond brick with vitrified headers, half-hipped tiled roof. Raised staddlestones[5]

Semington	Church Farmhouse, Church Street, Late C16, Altered and extended C17, Refronted C18 Lean-to extension C19 (page 105)
Semington	Chapel of St. George, Church Street. C15 and 1860 restoration C19 three light window. 1877 half octagonal Vestry. Two C19 windows, Octagonal pulpit. Inscribed stone from C13 (page 24)
Semington	St George's Church, Church Street, 17 monuments (tombs) in Churchyard C17 to C19 (page 98)
Semington	Nos. 26 and 27 Church Street. Mid C16 Wings probably late C16. Noted for quality of Woodwork. Rear C20 extension (page 109)
Semington	The Old Coach House, off Church Street. 1790s with C20 bow window. Rear has C20 casements (page 98)
Semington	Littleton Wood Farmhouse, Devizes Road. Circa 1500, extended C16 and mid C17 (page 99)
Semington	Littleton Green Farmhouse, Late C16, C17 South wing. C20 kitchen extension (page 99)
Semington	Barn approx. 75m. NW of Littleton Wood Farmhouse. Late C16, said to have been a chapel (No records or evidence)
Semington	Brook Cottage, High Street, Early C19 Railings and Gate Piers, Stables and Carriage House (page 100)
Semington	"Red Cross House", High Street, mid C19 Formerly known as the Parsonage. Tuscan Portico and fine staircase (page 101)

Semington	Semington House, High Street, 1794 inscribed at top of pilaster. Now divided into two parts - Number 29 and Semington House (page 101)
Semington	Brook House, High Street, circa 1850 (page 102)
Semington	The Somerset Arms, High Street, mid to late C18 (page 86)
Semington	"The Manor House", High Street, Datestone 1698 Late C17 walls and gate piers (page 102)
Semington	Nos. 69 and 70 High Street. Pair of cottages Mid C18, each with C20 door (page 103)
Semington	Highfield House, High Street. With railings and Gate late C18. Built as a farmhouse, twinned with Semington House across the road (page 103)
Semington	Littleton Mill House, Littleton Mill Lane Late C18 (page 104)
Semington	Littleton Mill, Littleton Mill Lane. C18. Rebuilt Early 1800s. Some C20 additions. With retaining Walls to weir sluices, probably late C18. Altered C19 and C20 (page 110)
Semington, now Hilperton	Church of St. Mary, Whaddon. C12, C14, 1770s Long Family Chapel. Chancel rebuilt 1879 Walls enclosing churchyard prob. mid.C19 Redman Monument in churchyard (page 18)
Semington	Built as Melksham Union Workhouse (1836-8) (Later known as St George's Hospital (page 178)

This list is not exhaustive: there are other buildings in Semington of similar age to those recorded above:

Above: Littleton Wood Farmhouse

Opposite above: Semington Aqueduct

Opposite centre: Table Tombs in the Churchyard

Opposite below: The Old Coach House. (Courtesy David Daniels)

Below: Littleton Green Farmhouse

Bridge House, formerly the toll-keeper's house on the Wilts & Berks Canal, is noted as being complete in 1802. Bridge House and the adjoining Newtown Farm were sold by auction in 1978 (page 140)

Canal Cottages (page 172)

The former Bell Inn in the High Street, opposite the Somerset Arms, appears to have been in existence since the early C18. The Will of William Stokes of Semington, dated 1710, bequeathed "his leasehold house and close in Semington... known as the sign of the Bell" to Elizabeth and Jane Stokes, daughters of John Stokes, of Semington, clothier. The adjacent cottages also date from about the same time (page 86)

Row of cottages in High Street (Nos. 11, 12 and 13). No. 12 recorded as Blacksmith's house (page 42)

No. 71 High Street (page 104)

Littleton Mill Farmhouse. Late 16th century. Altered late 18th century (pages 104, 110)

Brook Cottage

Red Cross House (Old Parsonage)

Semington House

Brook House

The Manor House

Nos. 69 & 70 High Street

Highfield House

Littleton Mill House

71 High Street

Littleton Mill Farmhouse

CHURCH FARM, SEMINGTON

Church Farm is about a hundred yards east of St George's Church and probably dates from the first half of the sixteenth century. The location and name are the only known connections with the Church. Its length is close to the north-south direction. When first built it seems to have been of simple construction, two rooms at ground level, with a hall-passage from the front door running between, two rooms above and a thatched roof. Later in the same century there seems to have been money to add at the north end a stone hearth and chimney and spiral stair (removed mid-20th century). A late Tudor stone front was put in place of the original wooden structure, and eventually a stone-built double gable was placed at the south end with late Tudor-style hearth and chimney. Around 1670 to 1680 a single gable extension was added at the back. The evidence for the date was an intact clay pipe found in the farthest corner of the single attic with a dateable heel-stamp and the maker's name, Buckland. At some stage the thatched roof was replaced with a second roof of shallower slope and stone tiles. The weight of the stone tiles required replacement in turn with lighter tiles and slates. At one period the house was divided, with two stairs and two front doors.

So far the earliest occupant of Church Farm to be found in Wiltshire Records Office was called Cox, from about 1790 to 1810, when the Duke of

Somerset acquired it. The purchase was probably related to the commercial possibilities arising from the completion of the Kennet and Avon Canal towards the east and the junction with the new Wilts and Berkshire Canal from the north.

From the Census returns it can be ascertained that the property, comprising some 100 acres, was being farmed by William White and his family from 1841 to 1881. In 1891 it was rented by William Glass, but the census return of 1901 records the house as uninhabited. By this time the Jefferys brothers, who had taken over Manor Farm in 1863, were jointly farming the land belonging to Church Farm

After the Duke of Somerset sold both farms in 1943 Church Farm was owned in turn by Tilley to 1948, Briden to 1954, Hulbert to 1964 (when the farm was sold, together with the homestead, a range of farm buildings, 60 acres of pasture and arable lands and a cottage at 552 Canal Terrace to a Mr Holton). In 1974, Edgeborough Building Co.Ltd. planned the demolition of the house but eventually sold it in 1977, to a Mr Norman. In 1982 it was bought by Dr Hugh McBryde.

From information supplied by the late Dr. Hugh McBryde in February 2002.

Granary at Manor Farm

MANOR FARM

According to the Census Returns, Manor Farm (then called Semington Farm) was occupied by Richard Pocock (farmer of 250 acres, aged 22) in 1841 In 1861 James Pocock was occupying Semington Farm (now with 315 acres and employing 13 men, 4 boys and 4 women) By 1871 William Jefferys had been at Semington Farm since 1863, farming 350 acres and employing 9 men and 3 boys.. In 1901 Jefferys was still renting what was now called Manor Farm, aged 59, with his wife, Anne, and his five children. His sons, William and Henry, later took over from him, working both Church and Manor Farms together until 1943, when both farms were sold by the Duke of Somerset. The two brothers retired a year later., the Jefferys family having rented Manor Farm for 81 years and Church Farm for 47 years.

When Manor Farm was put up for sale by auction in 1947 the house was described as a XVII Century Stone and Tiled Farmhouse and the farm was "noted for its well watered and prolific nature, being some of the very best land procurable in the Wiltshire Vales. The lands are level deep soil of an alluvial nature noted for their production of Milk or fattening of cattle and production of Market Garden and Corn Crops, of an easy working nature".

Manor Farm is still a working dairy farm, with 200 Friesian cows, 14 acres of grain and 30 acres of maize, used as silage. The calves are kept to be sold as beef.

The Granary (which is a listed building) is dated 1711 and is thought to be about the same age as the house.

Nos. 26 & 27 CHURCH STREET, SEMINGTON

These two houses are halves of a timber-framed and stone building, thought to be of the 15th or early 16th century. The whole house has a long hall range parallel to the road with two wings running north, one at either end. No. 26 includes the larger part of the hall range and the east solar wing and No. 27 the kitchen of the hall range and the west service wing. The portion of the hall range in No. 27 was part of the original house. The building is of great significance on account of its age and more especially for the quality of the woodwork in the main range and the survival of fireplace features and other details throughout. Photographs suggest that No. 26 was the upper part of the house and that it retains even finer mouldings, certainly brackets which supported oriel windows can be seen at first floor level on the east and west elevations of the east wing, which points to the room within having been the solar (solarium: built to catch the sun's rays).

Because of its size and position it seems reasonable to suggest that this building, although it has not yet been possible to trace all its history, might well have been the original Manor House of Semington. The earliest firm mention is in the Will of the Reverend. Richard Kitson, rector of West Tytherley, Hants., from 1596 to 1642, when he left all his "lands and tenements with the appurtenances in Semington . . . . . to my son John Kitson and his heires for ever". John Kitson, having fought on the wrong (Royalist) side in the Civil War (see Chapter 1) sold his property to John Twyford,. of Semington, in 1646. Thereafter it appears to have been owned by other members of the clergy, one of whom presumably bequeathed it to All Souls College, who were in possession by the time of the Commutation of Tithes map of 1837. The property was at that time occupied by Thomas Bruges and the whole estate was later bought by another member of the Bruges family in or just before 1877.

The above information has been extracted from the Wiltshire Buildings Record. Reference WILBR 1968.

No. 26 Church Street (above) and No. 27 Church Street

Opposite: Side view of No. 26

Littleton Mill from the air. (Courtesy S. Wills & R. Oglesby)

Littleton Mill Farmhouse: side view

Chapter 8

FARMING, FLORA & FAUNA, THE AVON HUNT

MY DAD

My Dad he was a country man, a family man
Down on the farm, a labouring man.
He worked all day from dawn to dusk,
To earn a pittance, he cared for us.

He'd rise at dawn throughout the seasons,
To call in the cows, Herefords and Friesians
Then to the sheds and washed ready for milking,
Daisy, Buttercup, all flowers, busy chewing.

When milking was finished, strained, cooled and churned,
The cows being turned out to graze,
My Dad came home for breakfast, fried bread, bacon and egg,
Two large cups of tea but no time to laze.

Back to the farm, there's so much to do,
Mucking out, swilling down, troughs to fill too,
Ploughing, drilling, sowing, took care of spring days,
Cutting and tossing, the smell of new hay.

Soon came the harvest, the gathering of corn,
Long days of hard work, weary and worn.
Dirty work, thirsty work, my Dad did it all.
Labouring with pride, standing straight and tall.

So many are the duties of a farm labourer,
Hedging and ditching in all sorts of weather.
Cutting and laying a hedge with great skill,
Sharpening his chopper on a stone, with a will.

Stone picking, potato picking, back breaking work,
Big chaps on his hands, how they must have hurt,
Bringing in turnips, swede and kale,
All to be used as animal fare.

The animals, I know, Dad loved them all,
The cows, the bull, the pigs, the boar,
He cleaned, fed and nursed them, helped with their birth,
For animals make the best friends on earth.

After tea, in the garden, and when he found time,
He dug, raked and sowed, and planted, like soldiers in line,
He gathered in food of all different kinds,
To feed all of us, his family, and mine.

The chicken hut too, had to be cleaned,
With water pulled up from the well,
Wood chopped and split, the coal scuttle filled,
The doors locked and the windows sealed.

The evening, to me, was the best of the day,
He'd sit by the fire and make rag rugs to lay,
By the light of the oil lamp, filled, primed and lit,
I'd sit on his knee and he'd read for a bit.

At home in the cottage, he was our dear Dad.
Bringing us rabbits for dinner and milk to be had.
Cowslips for Mum, mushrooms for tea,
I loved my Dad and I know he loved me.

Glenys Bright

FARMING

Thomas Davis, writing on Wiltshire Agriculture in 1811, noted that Wiltshire was capable of producing most of the essential products required for human sustenance and because of its soil being in good heart could produce far more than was needed for local consumption. These products included wheat and barley, milk products, calves, cattle, sheep and pigs. Large numbers of sheep were bred in the county and then sold off to be fattened elsewhere. A healthy wool trade followed from the store (kept locally) sheep. Tithes were mainly paid in kind.

Thomas Davis also provided a very good description of the building necessary for a Wiltshire farm, as follows: three barns or at least three thrashing floors, to avoid the mixing of grains, a barn on low stone pillars, to keep out rats and mice, for wheat storage; stabling for horses, a cow shed and yard for wintering cattle; granary, pigsties and a sheltered yard surrounded by buildings; a farmhouse giving a good view of the yard; a supply of drinking water in the yard for cattle.

Davis noted a particular problem with Wiltshire farmers: "They are too fond of putting their corn into barns instead of building ricks, with the result that the corn is damp and rough instead of dry and slippery."

Milking time, c. 1904. (Courtesy Mrs M. Gover)

The common field system was much used when small farmers co-operated to make better use of the land, so the common herd of cattle was restricted to an agreed area, away from growing crops. There were more enclosures in Wiltshire than in other Southern and Western counties.

Davis also recorded that until the 1790s it was normal for the landlord to pay all taxes. The poor rates then increased to such an extent that the landlords passed the burden of parochial taxes down to the tenants. This forced the tenants to hire labourers by the week as they were needed, so that the labourers did not become settled in the parish and become a charge on the parish rates.

The average weekly payments to the poor rates in agricultural parishes were from 2s. 6d. to 4s. in the £, whilst in manufacturing parishes the rate rose to between 7s. and 14s. in the £ on actual rents of the property.

Farming implements were horse drawn:

(a) the hill plough with two wheels and the point of the beam raised.

(b) the lowland plough with a single wheel which could be changed for a skid for wet ground use.

Both of these ploughs were about 8 feet long and fitted with a shaped board whose purpose was to upturn the soil lifted by the plough point.

Harrowing was normally performed by a trio of horses pulling three sets of discs fixed at an angle to the direction of travel, which effectively chopped into smaller pieces the turned up soil.

Carts were made deep and capacious so as to enable the maximum load of manure to be carried. Wagons could be used to carry manure, but if possible were kept clean for the transport of crops. The traditional Wiltshire wagon could be recognised by its having smaller diameter front wheels as compared to the rear wheels.

Wiltshire is still basically a farming county, with the exception of Swindon, which first came to notice as a "railway town" and, more recently, has evolved into an "industrial" would-be city. Swindon apart, the remainder of the county is dotted with market towns, plus the Cathedral City of Salisbury, with its surrounding villages. Salisbury is cut off from the Northern part of Wiltshire by the military area of Salisbury Plain, which is also extensively farmed.

Around the market towns lie dozens of villages, of which Semington is one. The distribution of the market towns was governed by the distance over which cattle could be driven on market days - say, 4 or 5 miles. For instance, within living memory cattle would be driven from Semington to Trowbridge market.

Because parish boundaries are changed from time to time it follows that whole farms or parts of farms get transferred to neighbouring parishes. Such an example is Whaddon, which was recorded as Semington but is now part of Hilperton parish.

Apart from Manor and Church farms the following farms have at some time been part of Semington (those marked with an asterisk are now in other parishes): Little Marsh, Brickfield, Strangers Corner, Newhouse, Paxcroft*, Littleton Wood, Littleton Green, Melksham Park, Newtown*, Outmarsh*, Whaddon Grove*, Whaddon*.

Mixed farming, c. 1904. (Courtesy Mrs M. Gover)

The farming carried out was and is mainly pasture with some arable, Wiltshire being divided into "Chalk" and "Cheese", and Semington being in the Clay Vale, therefore part of the "Cheese". However it remains to be seen what will happen to the livestock numbers following the problem in the year 2001 with "foot and mouth" disease, which, luckily, did not break out in Semington.

The general county-wide picture is of a green and wooded hilly landscape with hidden towns and villages. The upland farming is mainly sheep grazing.

In the nineteenth century all farm machinery was horse drawn and that meant that there was a limit to the amount a horse could pull. So the farm ploughs, reapers, binders, etc., were of lightweight construction and sometimes became broken, which meant that work had to stop until the village blacksmith could effect repairs. The use of horses also meant that each farm had stables for the horses and there had to be a stableman, responsible for seeing that the horses were fed and watered every day, including Christmas Day.

At harvest time every villager who was available was pressed into service, either to scythe, collect and tie sheaves, or to load carts. Even children helped by forming a circle and gradually driving rabbits to the centre of the field, where they could be caught and later eaten. The rabbits provided a welcome addition to the larder and were regarded as one of the perks of harvest time. Comments were sometimes made by neighbouring counties against each other: typically - "if it moves they in Wiltshire'll eat it".

The harvest activities were always followed by Harvest Festival Services (to give thanks for the crop) in the Chapels and Churches, which would be decorated with local produce.

Each farm had its own method of crop storage. Grain which had been separated from the husks and stems was normally stored in "close weave" sacks either in a covered barn or, as has been seen in Semington, in a "raised" barn (see "Listed Buildings" chapter) the husks and stalks either being used for animal feed or as fuel or packing in the local brickworks. Long stem crops, which were needed for hay, were baled and stacked in a convenient field corner. Some very large farms could afford to put a "thatched roof" over their haystacks.

The modern harvest is completely mechanised and is worked by two or three people who operate the entire process, from cutting/threshing to baling, to storage, either as open bales in an open-sided roofed barn, or as plastic-bagged bales in a field. Bagged or bulk grain is now either stored as before or kept in a modern silo, either on the farm or at a collection centre. The only horses to be seen on a farm nowadays are for riding purposes, unless a small team is kept for preservation events or ploughing contests.

MANOR FARM

This farm was acquired by the Duke of Somerset sometime in the late 18th century. In 1851 it was called Semington Farm and was occupied by Richard Pocock (aged 22, a farmer of 250 acres) and his wife Sarah. Ten years later James Pocock (aged 40), with his wife Mary and their seven children were

SEMINGTON
AFTER OVER 80 YEARS.

Messrs. Jefferys Leave Local Farms.

Lady Day marked the severance of the Messrs. Jefferys' farming connection with village of Semington, which has lasted for over 80 years. The brothers—Messrs. W. G. and H. S. Jefferys—with their father before them, had occupied the Manor Farm for 81 years and the Church Farm for 47 years. They are now entering on retirement, and in October last the farms were sold by auction by Messrs. Thompson and Noad, by instructions of the Duke of Somerset, the purchaser of both farms being Mr. L. E. Turner, of Widbrook Farm, Bradford-on-Avon.

The departure of the Messrs. Jefferys from the village is generally regretted. A correspondent writes :

There was quite a pathetic little gathering outside the Dairy at Manor Farm on Friday morning, on the retirement of Messrs. Jefferys Bros. The employees of W. G. and H. S. Jefferys presented the two brothers with a silver cigarette box and a silver tobacco box. The presentation was made by the oldest employe, Mr. C. Watts, and his heart almost got the better of his speech, for words were hard to find. He thanked the brother farmers for their kindness and generosity to all in the past, and wished them the very best of health and happiness in the future.

In thanking the employees very much Mr. W. G. Jefferys, on behalf of his brother and himself, referred to them all as pals and said he hoped they would all get on as well with their next master as they did with them.

And so the little gathering broke up and I for one, as an employe will never forget that 15 minutes.

Messrs. Jefferys Bros. also generously rewarded the employees, with more than five years service, with £10 each, and others according to their service.

The village of Semington will miss two of the most kind and generous gentlemen who have ever lived in it.

W.A.P.

Wiltshire Times: April, 1944

living there. They had increased the size of the farm to 315 acres and were employing 13 men, 4 boys and 4 women. In 1863 William Jefferys was in residence, and by the 1871 census had 350 acres and was employing 9 men and 3 boys. His sons, William and Henry, took over from him, working both Church and Manor farms together until 1943, when both farms were sold by the Duke of Somerset. The two brothers retired a year later, the Jefferys family having rented Manor Farm for 81 years and Church Farm for 47 years.

Several examples of prices ruling in 1944, from the sale by Messrs Thompson & Noad of items from Manor Farm, are given below:

Bartlett sack scales and weights	£11.10s.00
Single furrow plough	10s.10d.
Single shaft harvest waggon	£44.00.00
Hens	£1. 6s.00
Horse	76 guineas*
Jersey cow and calf	£75

(* 1 guinea = 21 shillings)

When Manor Farm was put up for auction in 1947 the house was described as a 17th century Stone and Tiled Farmhouse and the farm was "noted for its well watered and prolific nature, being some of the very best land procurable in the Wiltshire Vales. The lands are level deep soil of an alluvial nature noted for their production of milk or fattening of cattle and production of Market Garden and Corn Crops, of an easy working nature."

Manor Farm is still a working dairy farm, with 200 Friesian cows, 14 acres of grain and 30 acres of maize, used as silage. The calves are kept to be sold as beef.

The Granary (which is a listed building) is dated 1711 and is thought to be about the same age as the house.

CHURCH FARM

This farm does not appear to have been given its name until 1861, although William White had been its tenant since 1841. In 1851 he was farming 100 acres and employing 4 men and 1 boy. In 1881 it was being farmed by William Glass, but by 1901 the farmhouse itself was unoccupied and, as mentioned above, the Jeffreys brothers were working both Manor and Church farm together until they retired in 1944. The farm and homestead was sold by auction as a going concern in 1964, but the land appears eventually to have been redistributed amongst what was left of the farming community in Semington, leaving the house and its immediate surroundings to be acquired by the late Dr .McBryde in 1982.

"HIGHFIELD"

This small farm was put up for sale by auction in 1958 as a Freehold Dairy or Grazing Holding with Residence, which "stands well back from the main road, with Lawns in front, Walled Kitchen Garden and Ornamental Garden and Lawns at side and rear, with small Orchard containing a variety of good Fruit Trees, and is constructed of Brick and Stone, with Part Tiled and Part Slated Roof" and 23 acres of "healthy, rich sweet feeding pasture lands", in one field of which now stands the new village school, which was erected in 1967. Most of the land was sold for development, but "Highfield House" became a restaurant for some years, and is now privately owned.

OUTMARSH FARM

This "Cotswold Style Farmhouse of quiet charm" with extensive farm buildings, was for sale by auction in 1958 as a "renowned and attested dairy or grazing farm" in Semington, having an area of nearly 169 acres, and is still a working farm, although outside the current boundary of Semington.

FLORA AND FAUNA

With the exception of the birds and the fish the undermentioned information has been kindly supplied by Sally Scott-White, of Wiltshire Wildlife Trust.

The drawings are by Sylvie Lloyd.

FLORA

The rarer species of plants found in the Semington area include Arrowhead, Nuttalls Water Weed, Perfoliate Pondweed, Fig-leaved Goosefoot and Leopards Bane.

More common species are: Great and Lesser Burdock, Horse-radish, Black Spleenwort, Silver Birch, Many-seeded Goosefoot, Woolly Thistle, Hemlock, Swine Cress, Annual Wall-rocket, Teasel, Lady's Bedstraw, Reed Sweet-Grass, Wild Privet, Italian Rye-Grass, Honeysuckle, Crab Apple, Water Chickweed, Pale Persicaria, Curly Pondweed, Celery-leaved Buttercup, Wood Dock, Crack Willow, Hoary Ragwort, Black Nightshade, Prickly Sow-thistle, Smooth Sowthistle, Marsh Woundwort, Tansy, Goats Beard, Great Mullein, Horse Chestnut, Common Fleabane, Large-leaved Lime, White Bryony, Fern Grass, Hedgerow Cranesbill, Water Plantain, Lesser Water-Parsnip, Common Water-starwort, Lesser Pond-sedge, Rigid Hornwort, Canadian Waterweed, Tall Fescue, Meadow Cranesbill, Plicate Sweet-grass, Dames Violet, Yellow Iris, Greater Duckweed, Gipsywort, Water Mint, Yellow Water-Lily, Butterbur, Reed Canary-grass, Fennel Pondweed, Stream Water-Crowfoot, Common Club-rush, Branched Bur-reed, Lesser Stitchwort, Hop Trefoil.

FAUNA

Mammals: Bats, Brown Rats, Foxes, Grey Squirrels, Hedgehogs, Mink, Badgers, Moles, Rabbits, Stoats, Weasels, Water Voles, Deer, Wood Mice, Field Mice, Hares, Shrews, Water Rats.

Reptiles and Amphibians: Common Frogs, Grass Snakes, Eels

Butterflies: Comma, Green Hairstreak, Holly Blue, Purple Hairstreak, Common Blue, Marbled White, Large White, Red Admiral, Peacock, Tortoiseshell, Brimstone, Small White

Water and Marsh Birds: Herons, Mallards, Swans, Coots, Brent Geese, Moorhens, Kingfishers (now rare)

Clockwise from top left: Hemlock, Teasel, Honeysuckle, Fox, Grey Squirrel, Badger.

Clockwise from top left: Water Vole, Wood Mouse, Hare, Frog, Common Blue Butterfly, Marbled White Butterfly.

Clockwise from top left: Heron, Mallard, Swan, Kingfisher, Robin, Bullfinch

Birds: Robins, Sparrows, Blackbirds, Greenfinches, Bullfinches, House Martins, Swallows, Swifts, Barn Owls, Sparrowhawks, Thrushes, Starlings, Blue Tits, Longtailed Tits, Coal Tits, Great Tits, Magpies, Goldfinches, Dunnocks, Ring Doves, Spotted Woodpecker, Green Woodpecker, Fieldfares, Pheasants, Partridge (occasional), Redwing (occasional), Kestrel, Pied Wagtails, Yellow Wagtails, Wrens, Buzzards, Jays, Jackdaws, Tree Creepers, Cuckoos (heard in Spring only) Yellow Hammers, Chaffinch, Wood Pigeon, Skylark, Linnet, Crows, Rook, Jackdaw.

Fish: Freshwater Mussels, Eels, Pike, Tench, Bream, Roach, Perch in the Canal, and Brown Trout, Chub and Dace in Semington Brook.

Dragonflies: Brown Hawker, Southern Hawker, Migrant Hawker, Common Darter, Black-tailed Skimmer, White-legged Damselfly

Clockwise from top left: Barn Owl, Kestrel, Wren, Pied Wagtail

AVON VALE HUNT

The Avon Vale Hunt was for years quartered in Semington and in 1923 had 30 couples of hounds. The Hunt met on Wednesdays and Saturdays with an occasional bye day.[1] The only connection with the Hunt now remaining is the housing development situated near the former kennels and called The Hunt Close. Occasionally foxes can still be seen around and sometimes within the village.

Above: Avon Vale Hunt in Semington, 1924. (Courtesy Mrs M Gover)
Below: Former Hunt Master's house

During World War II the village of Semington adopted the Hunt Class Destroyer HMS *Avon Vale* in 1942. The destroyer survived the War and was finally scrapped at Sunderland in 1958.

HMS *Avon Vale* was a Hunt Class (TYPE 2) Escort Destroyer of 1,050 tons driven by two shaft geared turbines producing 19,000 shaft horse power, giving a top speed of 25 knots. It was armed with six 4-inch Anti-Aircraft Guns in 3 twin turrets and five 2 pounder A.A. guns (one quadruple and 1 single) plus two 20mm Oerliken guns. The ship had a crew of 168.[2]

References

1 From Kelly's Directory, 1923.

2 From Lenton, H.T., and Colledge, J. J., *Warships of World War II*, p. 127.

Hunt Close

IN THE MARKET FOR THE FIRST TIME FOR 150 YEARS

With VACANT POSSESSION on Completion

WILTSHIRE

THE HIGHLY ATTRACTIVE FREEHOLD

Riverside Country Mill Property

with planning permission for change of use to a distinctive house of character with land,

known as

LITTLETON MILL

Semington, Nr. Trowbridge.

FOR SALE BY AUCTION

at

THE TOWN HALL, MELKSHAM

on

WEDNESDAY 2nd FEBRUARY 1977

at 3 pm.

Auctioneers:

NOAD & SON

Clare House,
35 Market Place,
Melksham, Wilts.
(Tel: (0225) 703018

also at

39 Market Place,
Chippenham,
& Corsham, Wilts.

Solicitors:

MANN, RODWAY & GREEN

3 Market Street, Bradford-on-Avon, Wilts.
(Tel: 3138) also at Trowbridge.

Printed by Charles H. Woodward Ltd., Devizes.

Littleton Mill - Sale Document. (Courtesy R Oglesby)

Chapter 9

THE MILLS, BRICKYARD, ABATTOIR, TANNERY AND BOATBUILDING

THE MILLS

Semington Brook, which rises on Salisbury Plain, south of Bratton (some 15 kms – 10 miles – to the south of Semington) and joins the River Avon at Whaddon, has a source fed by springs which produce sufficient water all year round to support a series of mills, one of which, now known as Littleton Mill, is in the Parish of Semington. Cloth-makers in Semington, as in the West of England generally in the middle ages, were producing white broadcloth and this was being exported to Europe as a top-quality and expensive product.

It is mentioned in the Domesday Book that there were two mills in the Keevil area (which Arnulf de Hesdine held from the King) one of which may have been Littleton Mill, records of which go back at least to the Middle Ages. It had been a copyhold tenement of the Abbess of Romsey's Manor of Steeple Ashton since the 10th century. In 1495 it was let to Robert Long as a fulling mill for 95 years and after his death was taken over by another clothier, Anthony Passion, who by 1545 was one of the most prosperous men in the county. By the early seventeenth century the freehold had passed to the Somner family, various members of whom seem to have held it as clothiers for much of the century. When Thomas Somner died in 1699 ownership of the Mill descended through the Hippersley and Goddard families successively until 1780, when Ambrose Awdry owned it. In 1797 it was offered for sale, described as "a grist and fulling mill by a large and never-failing stream of water, with a considerable fall and great improvement". It was bought by Francis Naish, a major Trowbridge clothier, who let it to Ralph Heath.

In the early 1790s machinery had been introduced which displaced many thousands of workers. The "gig mill" and the shearing frame began to threaten the trade of the most skilled group of woollen workers, the shearmen or cloth dressers, who finished cloths prior to sale. These men were already highly organised into illegal but strong trade unions. In the law courts they sought to invoke old legislation from Tudor times, which prohibited the use of the gig mill. When eventually other sanctions failed they resorted to violence, firstly to minor acts of sabotage and then to assaults on the machinery itself and the mills that housed it. These "Wiltshire Outrages" alarmed the Government who sent numbers of troops to the area to protect the main mills.

At 1 a.m. on Thursday morning, 22 July, 1802, Littleton Mill, let to Ralph Heath, was attacked by a number of shearmen, who, armed with muskets, pistols and bayonets, were believed to have come from one of the mills at Trowbridge belonging to Francis Naish.. In the resulting melee the mill was burnt down, although no one appears to have been hurt. There were varying accounts about the amount of cloth having been burnt, but apparently Ralph Heath managed to save most of his own stock.

The local cloth manufacturers, under the leadership of John Jones, an important Staverton clothier, applied to the Government, who sent a London magistrate, James Read, of Bow Street, to take charge of the situation A £50 reward was offered for the bringing to justice of the ringleader. Thomas Helliker, a 19 year-old apprentice shearman or "colt" who worked in the finishing shops of Francis Naish in Trowbridge, was eventually identified by Ralph Heath as the person most actively concerned in the raid on the mill. After a trial, and despite his many protestations of innocence Helliker was found guilty and was hanged at Fisherton jail in Salisbury on 28 March 1803.

After the execution, which took place in front of some 3,000 people (mostly cloth workers, not only from local towns but even from Gloucester and Yorkshire) Thomas Helliker's body was placed on a cart by his fellow shearmen and taken across Salisbury Plain back to Trowbridge., where he was buried with full religious rites by the Curate (for which he was subsequently reprimanded by the absentee Vicar). The Tomb erected to the memory of Thomas Helliker can still be seen in the churchyard at St James's, Trowbridge. Later enquiries indicate that he was probably not the guilty person.

Ralph Heath never ran the mill again and it was sold in June 1803 to the Kennet and Avon Canal Company, who needed water from the brook to feed the canal - it was cheaper to buy up the mills rather than pay compensation for the loss of water. It was rebuilt as a grain mill and as Littleton Wood Mill, then Littleton Mill, was operated by the Noad family for 150 years.

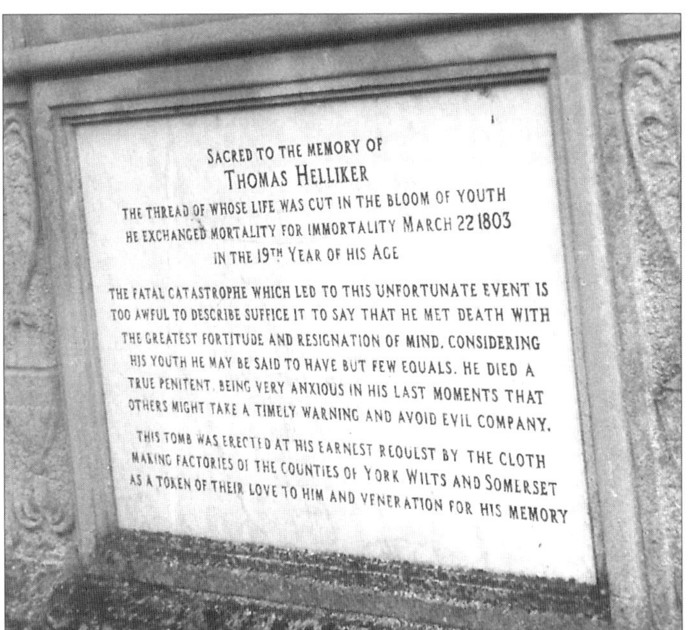

Tomb of Thomas Helliker

Noad family, about 1937. (Courtesy Mrs B Noad)

In the late 1930s the Noad family business was run by William Stephen, Henley, Joseph, George, H.T. (Tom), and Philip. By the late 1950s the family members concerned were Joseph, young James, George, Philip, Kingsley and Tom (H.T.)

Until 1932 grain originating from the Sea of Asov, Bessarabia, Morocco, Persia and the River Plate was transported to Littleton Mill from Avonmouth in barges named *Argus, Jenny* and *Jane*, carrying 500 sackloads per barge, each pulled by one horse (a three-day journey). These boats made a colourful sight with their painted and decorated cabins and are a happy memory to those who saw them.

ESTABLISHED OVER 100 YEARS

TELEPHONES:
HEAD OFFICE, LITTLETON KEEVIL 352
FLOUR MILLS, SEEND 246
BALDHAM MILLS, SEEND 287

Bought of **J. & J. NOAD**
Flour Millers
LITTLETON WOOD & SEEND HEAD MILLS
near TROWBRIDGE

PARTNERS
HENLEY T. NOAD
GEORGE P. NOAD
PHILIP NOAD
KINGSLEY J. NOAD

INVOICE

DISCOUNT TERMS
FLOUR
4d. in £ if paid strictly within 7 days of Invoice date.
3d. in £ if paid strictly within 14 days of Invoice date.
2d. in £ if paid strictly within 21 days of Invoice date.

Invoice Number and Date	*per 280 lbs.*	£ s. d.	£ s. d.

E. & O. E.

J & J Noad billhead

Seend Head Mill

The advent of motor transport caused the demise of the canal delivery system because one lorry could carry the same amount of grain in one day as the 500 bags brought by the barges, taking three days, and delivery came directly into the mill. This new supply route also ensured that the tramway and the canal wharf fell into disuse (see page 70). The Mill ceased to operate in 1977.

When Littleton Mill was converted to a private residence a number of items were given to Trowbridge Museum, but many distinguishing features remain, including the water turbine (which superseded the water wheel in 1926) which still operates and provides an electrical supply to the house. Wild fowl abound on the mill leet.

BRICKYARD

For a number of years Semington boasted its own brickyard at Penny Platt. The bricks produced had a distinctive orange colour when fired and were extremely hard, so much so that workmen frequently broke their tools when trying to cut or drill through them. No. 10 High Street, the house opposite the present village hall, was built using the local brickyard's product. A close inspection of the house, which was once the village shop and Post Office, will reveal that the front left-hand window, which was originally much larger, has been skilfully rebuilt.

Later the brickyard became a pottery, but when the clay seam at the brickyard was worked out, the hole in the ground remaining was used by the Avon Rubber Company as a disposal site for waste rubber. Periodically this rubber caught fire by spontaneous combustion. This necessitated the presence of the local fire brigade and the Avon Works Fire Brigade to extinguish the blaze. When these fires occurred considerable annoyance was caused to residents living to the north of the scene by the thick black smoke which hugged the ground as far as Melksham.

The number of people employed at the brickyard varied over time, according to the census returns[1] and various local directory entries:

In 1851	James Garratt (Brick and Tile Maker) employed 8 labourers
In 1861	James Garratt (Brickmaker) employed four men and two boys
In 1871	James Garratt (Brickmaker)
	Jeise " "
	John Perrett "
	James Heath "
In 1875	James Garratt (Brick and Tile Maker)
In 1901	Edwin Collins (Manager, Brickyard) employed three labourers
In 1903	Augustus Howell (Brickmaker)
In 1907	Charles Butt, Potter, Penny Platt
In 1911	Charles Butt, Potter, Penny Platt

After 1911 there is no further reference to either a Brickyard or a Pottery in the local directories held in the Wiltshire Record Office.

Semington brick. (Courtesy Mrs P Mortimer)

ABATTOIR

The abattoir is sited at what used to be the junction of the Kennet and Avon Canal and the Wilts and Berks Canal. The premises consist of the old W & B Tollhouse (see page 140), with the old stop lock buried in the garden, various outbuildings connected with the trade and a concrete yard which covers the original route of the canal. The continuation of the former canal northwards with its tree-lined route can be seen from the yard.

When agriculture changed over to tractors this made large numbers of horses redundant. Many of these horses were put down in Semington because abattoirs had to be licensed and they were few and far between. Therefore each abattoir served a large area of countryside. Being mostly farmland, worked by horse-drawn implements, Wiltshire had many more horses than other more urban counties.

The abattoir then dealt with farm animals until being forced out of business at the onset of the "BSE" scare in the 1990s.

TANNERY

There was once a tannery behind Canal Cottages, although there are no remains visible today; which would perhaps suggest that the tannery structures could have been built of wood.

The only record found thus far is in J. Pigot's 1830 *Commercial Directory*, where two names - that of Edward and Francis Naish, of Semington, are listed under "Tanners". As this information was collected prior to publication of the Directory it seems probable that the tannery existed in the 1820s or even earlier.

Before Semington had an independent entry under its own name, previous recordings in local directories came under the heading of Melksham and in 1783 there is recorded "Melksham - Tanner - ... Chapman". As the tannery location was adjacent to the canal junction, did the tannery exist to provide leather for canal boat use, bearing in mind that the barges were horse-drawn and this gave a requirement for general saddlery?

Further trades directories issued in 1842 and after do not record a tanner's business in Semington .

Kenneth Rogers, in his *Wiltshire and Somerset Woollen Mills*,[2] records:

Semington
A dye-house with two coppers, six vats, and a fire-stove with a dwelling house nearby, the property of Maurice Jarvis of Trowbridge, apothecary, was offered to let in 1746. In 1764 it was occupied by John Ledyard the younger.
[Ref: *Bath Journal* 9.6. 1746: WRO 947 - Jarvis Deeds]
NB: A Maurice Jarvis was Chapelwarden of Semington in 1744 and for some years afterwards

ARMS OF THE WORSHIPFUL COMPANY OF COACH AND HARNESS MAKERS.

BOAT BUILDING IN SEMINGTON

Reference to local Trades Directories during the 19th century gives the following information regarding boat builders in Semington:

Directory	Date	Name	Occupation
Pigot's	1822-3	Nothing at Semington	
Pigot's	1830	Nothing at Semington	
Pigot's	1842	John Theobalds Jnr	Boat Builder & Timber Merchant, Semington Lock
Kelly's	1848	W. Large	Boat Builder Semington Dock, Melksham

Slater's	1852-3	William Large	Boat Builder, Semington Road, Melksham
Kelly's	1875	Fras. Large	Boat Builder, Semington Road, Melksham
Kelly's	1880	Fras. Large	Boat Builder, Semington, Melksham
Kelly's	1895	Nothing at Semington	

NOTE: It seems likely that the John Theobalds of 1842 is the same John Theobald (sic) recorded as a Corn Merchant in 1852-3

References

1 From Census Returns from 1851 to 1901 in WRO and Kelly's Directories from 1898 to 1911 in Wiltshire Reference Library.

2 Rogers, Kenneth, *Wiltshire and Somerset Woollen Mills,* 1976, p. 111.

Covered Dry Dock

Bottom Lock & Lock Keeper's House

Chapter 10

THE CANALS AND THE RAILWAY

CANALS

THE KENNET & AVON

The Kennet and Avon Canal opened over its full length, from Reading to Bath, in 1810, sections at either end of the canal having been opened previously. The Act of Parliament allowing its construction had been passed in 1794.

The junction of the two canals - the Kennet and Avon and the Wilts and Berks at Semington provided a convenient place for changing horses, hence grazing land and stables were necessary. This junction also made for a sensible business site for boat building and repairs. There followed much later (in the 1970s) the construction of a covered dry dock entered from the Kennet and Avon Canal between locks and adjacent to the K & A Lock Keeper's house

The entrance to the Wilts and Berks Canal was just below the two Semington locks (See section on Wilts and Berks Canal). Just east of Newtown Farm Swing Bridge was a small wharf connected to Littleton Mill by a horse-drawn trolley on rails. This permitted the mill owners to bring bagged grain from Avonmouth/Bristol by barge to Semington, unload the bags at the wharf on to the trolley, which was then push-started to roll freewheel down to the mill. Later the unloaded trolley was drawn back up to the wharf by horse. Physical evidence of the rail track has long disappeared but some scant remains of the wharf can still be seen (see page 70). When the mill was not working this trolley became a source of attraction for local children, who would "ride the rails" until chased off by the owners.

During World War II the Kennet and Avon Canal formed the basis for a defence line of pillboxes, several of which were sited in Semington and a few derelict versions remain today (see page 150).

The Kennet and Avon Canal fell into disuse as cargoes were transferred to the railways and to road vehicles and the canal closed in 1932 after a number of years of casual use. The canal was re-opened in 1990, largely by the efforts of the K & A Preservation Trust. There are now increasing numbers of boats of various types, from the occasional working barge, numerous pleasure and houseboat conversions, hire boats of all kinds, canoes (there is an annual Devizes to Westminster canoe race) and the canal is also a popular venue for fishing contests. The towpath is used by walkers and cyclists and nearby villages, including Semington, are benefiting from the seasonal trade generated by the re-opening.

When the K & A canal was in full use goods for Semington were unloaded at Semington Wharf where the canal was widened to form a small basin and the Wharf Cottage was built in the 18th century (see page 94).

For a number of years during the 1970s and 1980s the Kennet & Avon Navigation Company Limited ran a broad beamed canal barge, the *Joseph Priestley*, for party hire, sailing between Semington and Trowbridge.

The boat is described as luxuriously appointed, with central heating, flush toilets with h & c running water, a bar and a sophisticated galley. The brochure gave private hire charges (per hour, including bar) as:

Daytime (10 am to 6 pm) October to March £10, April to September £12
Evenings (6 pm to 1 am) October to March £12, April to September £15
Catering and departure times by arrangement.

In the year 2002 a new traffic diversion around Semington involves the construction of a new aqueduct a short distance to the east of Semington top lock. The new aqueduct will mean that Semington and Melksham Without parishes will share two aqueducts. Is this unique for a pair of adjoining parishes?

WILTS & BERKS CANAL

The Act of Parliament for the creation of the Wilts and Berks Canal was passed in 1795 and given Royal Assent.

In 1799 it is recorded that the junction with the Kennet and Avon Canal had been completed together with the regulating lock or stop lock .and masonry bridge to carry the Kennet and Avon towpath over the Wilts and Berks Canal. The stop lock served two purposes: (a) it caused barges physically to stop for toll collection and (b) it meant that the Wilts & Berks canal was 1ft. 8ins above the K & A at this point. That stopped any legal case whereby the Wilts & Berks could be charged for taking water from the K & A, which itself had water supply problems. (A similar stop lock system was in use at the Dundas junction with the Somerset Coal Canal.)

This canal ran for 52 miles from Semington to Abingdon in Berkshire via

Entrance to W & B Canal, c.1910. Source untraced. (Courtesy of Mrs June Fry)

Swindon with branches to Chippenham and Calne en route. Because the canal was meant only for narrow boats it was possible to economise in the construction dimensions as compared with the K & A. The depth had to be kept to 4'6", the same as the K & A, or else the deeply laden barges carrying coal would have run aground. But the width was reduced to 27 ft and locks were only single width (about 7'3") and single-gate type, as compared with the K & A, which has double width locks and double gates..

There were no navigable rivers in the area except the Severn, the Thames and the Avon, from the River Severn to the City of Bristol. The only "main road" was the Bath Road, now known as the A4, from Bath to London, which was used by pack horses and mail coaches, whose average speed was 7 mph.

Construction commenced in 1795 and lasted for fifteen years with the connection being made to the Kennet and Avon Canal at Semington in 1799. Local clay was used to make the bricks used in the construction of bridges, locks, etc. These bricks were larger than the standard size brick (700 canal bricks being equal to 1000 common bricks). This was for tax avoidance purposes! (the tax being per brick produced). The first brickyard was at Melksham, with the next at Pewsham. The last bricks at each yard were used to construct the kilns at the next. Each bridge used over 30,000 bricks with the locks using nearly 200,000 and over 400 cu. ft. of stone. Lock gates cost £12.12s. for a single gate type (this included installation).

Three years later, in 1802, the Minutes of the Wilts and Berks Committee of Management[1] stated that the Toll Collector's House at Semington was complete. Note the height of this house (3 floors). This enabled a view along the K & A canal from the front top windows and a view along the W & B from the rear top windows. These views permitted the keeper to arrange barge movements in and out of the W & B canal so as to lose least water.

W & B Toll Collector's House

A further eight years elapsed (1810) before the canal was linked to the River Thames at Abingdon. At this time over 500 tons per week of Somerset coal was being transported via the Somerset Coal, K & A and the Wilts and Berks Canals to points further afield.

In 1814 the Toll Collector at Semington was paid £54. 12s. per annum. This rose to £70 in 1835. The lock keepers were paid an average wage of £36 per annum.

In the early 1840s the construction of the Great Western Railway at Swindon caused the amount taken in tolls to increase, but this only lasted for a few years. The railway was the cause of the decline in canal usage which followed from the opening of the G.W.R. from Bristol to London on 30th June 1841, running alongside the Wilts & Berks from Abingdon through Swindon to Chippenham.

The Somerset Coal Field at Camerton could not supply enough coal for the wants of customers on the Wilts & Berks because much more coal was being used by the Kennet & Avon customers. At the time of peak usage there could be up to 20 boats waiting to be loaded at Timsbury destined for the W & B.

The Wilts and Somerset Railway opened in 1848 from Chippenham to Westbury via Melksham, with a branch to Frome, allowing Radstock coal to be "exported" by rail and less being available to the Somerset Coal Canal and the K & A and the W & B.

In 1850 the Toll Collector at Semington had his salary reduced from £70 to £54.12s. and in 1851 it was further reduced to £46.16s per annum. The Canal Company was obviously in financial difficulties and new owners took over in 1877. Some goods were still being carried between Semington and Swindon, but elsewhere traffic was almost non-existent.

In 1888 the canal again had new owners, and for a few years all seemed well, with 1,327 tons being carried between Semington and Wantage in the mid-1890's. This position was not maintained, however, and in 1896 new owners again took over, and failed. Further use of the W & B could not be financially justified and in 1914 Parliament authorised the transfer to Swindon of the local section of the canal, and the abandonment of the remainder. Just 110 years had elapsed between the two Acts of Parliament.

FROM 1914 TO 2002

Various landmarks survive to mark the course of the former Wilts and Berks Canal. These include various building work remains, milestones and some sections of the canal, a few of which contain water. Even in Melksham it is possible to trace the route of the canal amongst the housing.

The southernmost mile and a quarter (two kilometres) is clearly visible

Same view as that on page 139, with blocked off Wilts and Berks Canal

and the Toll Collector's house at Semington is in perfect condition and lived in. The actual masonry arch bridge carrying the K & A towpath over the Wilts & Berks canal has been demolished and the spot marked with a semi-circular dummy arch in the retaining wall, and also, more recently, by the erection of a commemorative plaque on the K & A towpath above the original Wilts & Berks junction with the K & A.

When the Kennet & Avon Canal was partially drained in the year 2001 it was possible to see the entrance channel into the Wilts & Berks Canal as it had been cut over 200 years previously.

The 1990s have seen the formation of a Wilts & Berks Canal Restoration Group who are making progress with cleaning some obstructed sections and planning the re-routing of other sections which have been built over. It does not seem possible that the original junction with the K & A at Semington can be resurrected and currently possibilities to find a new route are being investigated.

SEMINGTON AND THE GREAT WESTERN RAILWAY

The Holt Junction to Devizes line opened on 1st July 1857 as a direct link without any intermediate stations, Some people travelled all day backwards and forwards between Holt and Devizes celebrating the arrival of the "Iron Horse". Gradually, in later years, various additional stops were added as villagers were encouraged to travel by the "new railway". Seend Station opened in September 1858. In 1862 the Devizes to Hungerford section was opened and it then became possible to travel from Holt to London via Devizes. The 1901 National Census records one Charles Edwards, of High Street, Semington, being employed as a railway platelayer. Semington Halt opened on 1st October 1906, the day that "God brought His Wonderful Railway" to Semington.

Semington Halt itself was on an embankment half a mile to the north of Semington towards Melksham. This embankment kept the railway track above the nearby River Avon flood level. Flooding in this area used to be a regular occurrence but, thanks to new methods of releasing water downstream, flooding is no longer the major problem it used to be.

The fact that the track was on an embankment necessitated building a bridge to carry the railway over the earth-surfaced Semington to Melksham Lane and the adjacent Wilts & Berks Canal.

Semington Halt. Photograph by D. J. Hyde, by kind permission of Rod Priddle (from GWR To Devizes*)*

All that can be seen of the remains of Semington Halt

G.W.R. (3141)

PICK UP WAGON No. 287

HOLT JUNCTION TO PADDINGTON

TO PICK UP AT

Seend, Patney & C., Woodborough, Pewsey, Savernake, Bedwyn, Hungerford, Kintbury.

3

TRAINS :-

5-5 p.m. ex Holt Junction to Newbury
3-15 p.m. ex Penzance—Newbury to Paddington

Date__________194 Truck No.__________

500 1/40.

Goods Label. (Courtesy of Desmond Clarke)

Horse & Cart. (Courtesy of "Steam", Swindon)

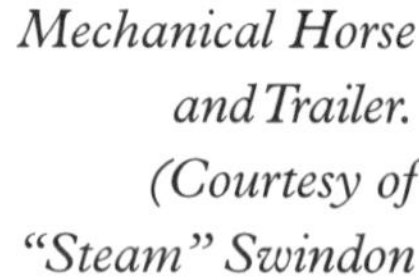

Mechanical Horse and Trailer. (Courtesy of "Steam" Swindon

Bridge at Semington. Photograph by kind permission of John Sawtell. (From GWR To Devizes*)*

To stop a train at Semington the prospective passenger had to raise their hand and give a clear signal to the driver. Passengers wishing to alight from the train had to inform the guard beforehand. Only pedestrian traffic could use Semington Halt as there was no vehicular access. But the station provided an easy means of getting to Devizes, Trowbridge, Westbury, or even London, especially in bad weather. All freight destined for Semington was delivered by road from Holt junction by horse and cart until the 1940s, the design of the cart, in having smaller diameter front wheels, enabled them when swivelled to pass beneath the body of the cart, thus making for good manoeuvrability when operating in confined spaces, such as goods yards. The horse and cart was replaced by the three-wheeled "mechanical horse", with its articulated trailer, a clever design which retained the ability to work in places with restricted room. Getting between the Halt and Semington village was often a hazard as regular flooding at the 13th century Brook Bridge at Semington would occur after heavy rain. This bridge was rebuilt and widened in 1947. The pagoda-type shelter at the Halt was on the left side of the road going towards Melksham, on the embankment above the cottages.

The bridge at Semington was just one of the major bridgeworks on this 12-mile stretch of line, others being at Whaddon, over the River Avon, at Foxhangers over the Kennet and Avon Canal, also at Caen Hill, Devizes, over the Trowbridge to Devizes Road. The majority of the track for its first ten miles from Holt is on a man-made embankment. These facts alone ensured that the project to build a rail link from Holt to Devizes must have been one of the more expensive branch lines in terms of construction costs.

The line was single-track except for a passing loop at Seend. This was sited at Seend not just because it was approximately the mid-point of the branch but also because the Seend Ironworks (now worked-out) were nearby and became connected to the railway system by a works tramway, so that as well as the passing-loop, there was a siding system for iron ore transfer from tramway to railway wagon.

Semington Halt platform was built using railway sleepers in 1906 when the small shelter was constructed. The platform structure was lower than standard height and this required the guard on the train to operate a lever to swing out a set of steps to enable passengers to climb aboard or to leave the train. This system sometimes caused a problem because if the guard forgot to retract the steps when the train reached a station with standard height platforms the steps would hit the platform and become damaged.

The locomotives operating the Holt-Devizes-Patney and Chirton service

Dean Goods Loco without Tender, (Courtesy of "Steam", Swindon)

57xx Class Locomotive (modified). (Courtesy of "Steam", Swindon)

Cornish Riviera Express 1961. (Photograph by Desmond Clarke)

have included firstly the steam railcoach (a coach with a steam propulsion unit built into one end) with a rear end driving compartment for reverse working. These were followed by 14xx class 0-4-2 Tank Engines (this numbering system indicating the wheel arrangement using a three-figure notation for leading wheels - driving wheels - trailing wheels) with converted steam railcoaches (the steam unit removed and replaced with seating) still with the rear control position which enabled push-pull working or, to use its official classification "auto-train working". This configuration eliminated the need to turn the locomotive on a turntable, the locomotives in question being fitted with a mechanical rod and lever link system between the locomotive and the rear control position on the coach. The driver being able to control the train from either end according to the direction of travel (the driver always being at the front)

The next type of locomotive to operate the auto-train system was the 57xx class 0-6-0 Pannier Tank, this class having a superior pulling power, which became necessary to haul heavier trains up the Devizes bank. These locos ran the service until closure with occasional relief operating by other random-type engines, including diesels.

Goods could be transported to a regular and known time-table, everything from a packet or parcel taken by the guard, to larger consignments in individual company-owned wagons, such as Wadworth's Brewery, Devizes Sand, local Coal merchants, as well as numerous colliery and nationally-known companies like Shell and Esso Petroleum, Fyffes Bananas, Saxa Salt, all in wagons prominently displaying their owners' name and business. The Holt to Devizes branch was also used for emergency working if alternative routes were blocked for some reason (such as a landslip) and for special tours. The Cornish Riviera Express is shown approaching Holt having previously passed through Semington as a result of the Lavington subsidence of 1961 (see page 146).

Considerable traffic used the branch line during the Second World War. Many RAF personnel travelled to and from Semington Halt in preference to Seend or Melksham Stations. Perish the suggestion that this was because Semington Halt was unmanned. To use Seend or Melksham Stations meant purchasing a ticket, something to be avoided if possible when Service pay was but 28 shillings per week less stoppages.

The Second World War also saw an increase in freight and military train working with a variety of engines including some on loan from other rail companies. To cope with heavier train loads some bridges, including Semington, had to be strengthened. Of course, heavier train loads also required

Above: Motorised Trolley. (Courtesy of "Steam", Swindon

Right: Bus waiting in Holt Station Yard, c. 1961. Photograph by Desmond Clarke

Semington Bridge Removal, 1969. Photograph by kind permission of John Sawtell. (From GWR To Devizes*)*

locomotives with greater pulling power and various classes of 2-6-0 , 4-8-0, 2-8-0 and 2-10-0 types were frequently to be seen working the branch line.

Track maintenance was originally by work gangs (hence the name "railway gangers") who walked the line and did necessary work when required, using equipment that they carried with them.

As a first improvement to that method of operation a small flat four-wheeled trolley was introduced for moving the equipment, much of which was quite heavy. The trolley was propelled by what appeared to be a see-saw fitted on top of the flat platform. Two men pumped the see-saw arms up and down and a linking mechanism to one axle moved the trolley along.

A further improvement was later introduced. This was a motorised trolley fitted with seats and electric spotlights. This permitted track inspection at night, at times when there was no passenger traffic and hence no train delays were caused. Some outlying villages were connected to major stations by a bus service. The bus would wait in the station yard for the arrival of a passenger train.

For the last few years before closure some of the stopping services were operated by diesel locomotives but the trains, which by then were made up with several coaches, had to retain one auto-coach per set so that passengers could alight from and board at the halts with low-level platforms.

The last train on the line was the 7.36pm diesel multiple unit from Newbury to Westbury on Monday the 18th April, 1966. All stations on the line were officially closed by railway reorganisation on the 19th April 1966: Holt Junction, Semington Halt, Seend, Bromham and Rowde Halt, Devizes, Pans Lane Halt, Patney and Chirton.

The tracks were soon lifted except for a short spur at the Holt end which was used at one time as an overnight stop for the Royal Train. Very little of the actual railway remains today. Many of the embankments and bridges have gone, (some with road-widening) for example, Caen Hill and Semington. The platforms at Seend are still visible, but there is nothing left of Devizes Station (now a car park).

Part of the eastern bridge buttress at Semington can be seen when the creeper covering is cleared away and the footpath leading up to where the platform was sited can just about be discerned, although mostly covered in a forest of weeds. The railway embankment at Semington is visible in both directions, although this is soon to be cut away about 200 metres to the east of the former Semington Bridge to allow the construction of the Semington-Melksham diversion road (see chapters on Maps and The Future).

Reference

1 From *The Wilts & Berks Canal*, by L. J. Dalby page 13

Remains of eastern bridge buttress at Semington

Pillbox (Blockhouse)

Chapter 11

REMINISCENCES

FROM A RESIDENT OF SEMINGTON

The Town on the stream. The stream known as Semington Brook starts at Lavington and joins the river Avon near Whaddon. It keeps its name from start to finish. Whaddon at one time was in the parish of Semington. The village area reaches from Whaddon to Seend.

Billy Bolwell! Yes, he kept some milk cows and could be seen carrying two pails of milk through the village on yokes. He supplied the villagers with good wholesome milk. No wonder they were tough and hardy. There used to be a blacksmith's shop opposite the old school near St George's Church and another one in the centre of the terrace houses opposite the Village Hall (see Chapter on Population. Occupations & Housing)) was kept by a Mr Fiveash, a very clever man who made his own tools of the trade. Near his house and the Wesleyan Chapel stood quite a large building called "The Tabernacle", perhaps a place of worship in the long gone past but then used as his workshop. As in life there is death, so the carpenter was also the local undertaker: no doubt he was never redundant.

A notable sight in the past was the three teams of shire horses from a local farm and their carters going to work near the Trowbridge Road. It was a very sad day when it was heard that one of the carters had collapsed and died behind his ploughing team. It was indeed "The Last Furrow". Another old time person was Mr S W Bailey, a farmer and qualified Veterinary Surgeon. He used to play the double bass and must have taken part in some entertainment. Being the man he was, many a person would go to him for advice.

One person of the village was Tramper. Who was Tramper? He was a chap who could not settle down and lived a rough life, having his mind disturbed through service in the first World War. Another character was Truefull Charlie. He and his wife were caretakers of the old village school. They both rode tricycles. He would tell tales of his service in India and was said to be able to talk Hindoo - more likely "double dutch". Another old chap who rode a tricycle was drainer Harvey. He was very conspicuous with his battered old hat and his corduroy trousers tied below the knees, making what was known as "yorks".

Wilts Rifle Volunteer Corps 1868. (Courtesy of Alf Curtis (Junior))

In the vicinity of the village there was a rifle range, mainly used by the old time Wiltshire Yeomanry. In the second World war it was used by the Home Guard to learn how to use a rifle (see page 70). During the 1939-1945 War Semington played its part in providing part of the Third Line of Defence against any invader by an excavated tank trap, concrete bollards and blockhouses. Also recesses were made in the Main Road to insert steel girders to pull off the tracks of invading tanks. Farmers were compelled to put farm machines by the roadsides ready to make road blocks to stop the invaders.

Bringing the Kennet and Avon Canal at the early part of the 19th century through the village must have brought industry, as there was once a thriving brickworks owned by Lord W H Long, MP and coal would have been brought from the Somerset coalfields to the Docks or Wharf near Semington Bridge. There was also imported timber from Russia and Canada to be transported to various places on the way to Reading and London

In the 19th century the woollen mills at Trowbridge needed a tremendous amount of water from the Biss river, so to supplement the supply a pumping station was built at Semington Brook to pump water through an underground pipe to Paxcroft Brook, then on to Trowbridge. Many hundreds of tons of imported grain must have been brought from Bristol to supply Littleton Mill.

In the 1930s there was a little shop in the old Manor House opposite the garage. It was kept by Alice Hancock : 'Granny' Hancock and her family. They also kept petrol pumps across the road from the shop. The landlord of the Somerset Arms also kept petrol pumps. All the pumps had an overhead

Wedding showing Pumping Station. (Courtesy of D. Barnett). *(See also page 70)*

Petrol pumps on both sides of road. (Courtesy of David Daniels)

pipe to fill thirsty vehicles so as not to obstruct the pavement. There must have been friendly rivalry between the two owners.

The boys of the village used to make a beeline to Granny's shop to buy 'bombers', being two pieces of metal joined together by a piece of string and costing a halfpenny, also to buy a halfpenny box of caps, being the ammo to go between the two pieces of metal to make a loud bang when dropped on a hard surface. It was a must for the lads to come away from the shop with a halfpenny packet of sweets, piled high by generous 'Granny'. These same boys used to borrow a long skipping rope from their school to pull stranded vehicles from the flooded roadway by the brook bridge. This road was subject to flooding until an obstruction was removed from the stream at Whaddon.

The now disused old road to the Semington Roundabout from Devizes consisted of a fairly steep hill. In its time it was certainly called Ragged Smock Hill. This seems to confirm an old story of there being an old windmill resembling an old chap wearing a tattered old coat.

Did any pirates live at Semington? On the left of St George's church door in the graveyard there is a tomb showing the "Jolly Roger" - that is, the skull and crossbones. It probably has some connection with a seafaring person.

Semington used to have its own little rail station, Semington Halt. The whistle of the trains when approaching and the chuff chuff when leaving, what lovely sounds. Perhaps if our ever-moving times had brought the diesel locomotive a little earlier our train service could still be here.

As still now, people had dry throats. In the past a popular beverage was local-made cider. One farmer had three cider presses made by his father and they went round the surrounding area making cider from the orchards on the farms. A thing of the past are those apple orchards, which at one time were a marvellous sight when in flower in the spring..

An old character of the village was Isaac Gulliver. He could be seen taking a young member of his family to the village school in the 1930s. He would always be seen wearing a snow white milking coat and walking with his thumb stuck out. He may have been associated with agriculture in some way, perhaps owning a little field and in his way felt himself an important person. It is said that an Isaac Gulliver was a smuggler, perhaps his grandfather. A family of the same name but no close connection moved to the Manor House in the thirties from The Strand.

In the past the Avon Vale Fox Hounds were kept at Semington. They were penned on land now occupied by the Industrial estate. When it was time for them to be fed, their baying could be heard from quite far away. It was a kind of music. They were often exercised on the main roads, something that would not be attempted today.

Before the 1939-45 War the Manor and Church Farms, then owned by the Duke of Somerset, were farmed by the Jefferys brothers, well respected gentlemen farmers. Many residents of Semington had someone in their family employed by them. There was a time when a field, now occupied by free range poultry, was folded by sheep and when ploughed the long, straight and tidy rows of stooked corn was a lovely sight to behold. Later on they would be taken back to the farm. In years gone by everyone when in Semington would at some time have heard the busy hum of some machine working. It was the threshing machine, driven by a steam traction engine, threshing corn from the immaculately stacked and thatched ricks of corn.

It may not occur to some that a valuable commodity passes through Semington 24 hours a day, namely through the fields in a section of underground pipe, part of the line from Fawley to Severnside. When first installed it carried ethylene chemical used in cloth-making but is now believed to carry oil. The line is regularly checked for defects by a helicopter which can often be seen flying over the route of the underground pipe..

In severe frost the canal east of the bridge would be used for skating by both young and old, with no accidents. Now prohibited for safety - still a loss of a pleasant recreation. A common form of footwear years ago for young lads were the hob- and brad-nailed boots worn when there was ice about. At the bottom of the field near the church was 'Glass's Pond', named after a one-time occupant of Church Farm. This pond could be described as a miniature lake and ideal for the boys' sliding sport. When the ice was thick and bearable, Harry Jefferys, the farmer, would with his pocket knife cut a hole to see how thick, or more likely to see if there was a hollow underneath, in which case it would be dangerous. Sometimes a frightening crack would be heard from the ice. "Only a safety crack!" someone would say. There was more clear space on the ice afterwards.

How many years ago? When preaching at the chapel the preacher in his enthusiasm on a passage in the Bible: "And the winds came and rooted them up", was waving his arms about and consequently knocking all the candles, etc., from besides his rostrum. Would it have been the same preacher? At a later time, when referring to the times that were gone, said: "They talk about the Good Old Times. Thank God they are gone".

The question now is what will the future times be like.

G.L.N.

MY YOUNGER DAYS

by Betty Bennett

I was born on the 10th February 1928 during a terrific thunderstorm, so my Mum always told me. My first memory at two and a half years was watching the midwife bathe my sister, Margaret. She dropped the corner of the towel in the bath water and I can remember her saying: "Oh, drat that".

Our childhood was spent surrounded by animals. My parents had a smallholding with pigs, goats, poultry, ducks and a pony. There was always plenty to keep us busy and amused. We would often have to wrap baby pigs in old woollies and put them close to the fire, because they would be chilled outside. We would watch them change from mauve to pink as they recovered, and would then return them to their mother in the sty.

Haymaking was a busy time, and quite unique! My father bought the grass on the canal bank, close to our house, up to a distance of two miles from home. He would cut it with a hand-held scythe. When it was dry he made small haycocks, ready for collection by a barge, pulled by Kit, our pony. This was very exciting for my sister and myself as we would ride in the barge to receive the hay and trample it down to make sure we could get it all in! There was often a gathering of on-lookers. Some helped us. It was very tricky bringing the barge through two sets of locks to the pound where the hay was unloaded on to a cart and taken to our yard, where father built his hayrick. By the time we were teen-agers our pony had died, so Dad decided we could take Kit's place, both pulling the barge and in the shafts! We managed very well, much to the amusement of some of the on-lookers. It was great fun and once the barge was moving it wasn't so much hard work. The cart had no brakes, so we had to run down the hill to our gate, but we always managed to manoeuvre the cart into the yard without overturning it!

We went to the village school. My mum had taught me how to write the alphabet. When I arrived home I would spend my time "teaching" my sister, whether she wanted to learn or not! School was mostly the "Three Rs" although we did some artwork, like sketching. Making new covers for our poetry books was done by potato printing. A slice was cut from a potato, which would then be carved into shape and dipped into paint and used as a printer. We did some PE. The boys particularly enjoyed this, as most of them had hobnail boots. "Astride and together" the teacher would say. The noise was deafening as the hobnails crashed to the concrete!. We were told to raise our knees on a level with our hips and the teacher would demonstrate and the

Mrs Betty Bennett and her younger sister. Courtesy of Mrs Betty Bennett.

boys could be heard to say: "pink ones today" as we all had a glimpse of her underwear, which was knee-length. We only had two teachers for the whole school. One took the 4 to 8 year olds and the other 8 to 14 year olds. They were expected to cover a lot of subjects. We played rounders in the Church Field during the summer and shinty and volley ball in the playground. There were no opportunities for cooking or woodwork, as there were no facilities. The Vicar, the Reverend Yerburgh, came from Steeple Ashton to teach on Thursday mornings. I can still remember the Catechism, which he insisted we learnt. Being a Church school, we had a Bible reading every morning.

When the 1939 war broke out the girls were all knitting for the Forces. We were allowed to knit during Scripture, as we called it. I managed a balaclava helmet every other day, as I also did knitting at home. Our classes enlarged overnight with the arrival of evacuees from London. They took over the Wesleyan Chapel schoolroom, with their teacher, Miss Watson.

During wartime my father was Chief Fire Warden for Semington. He distributed tin hats and axes. I remember joining him on the Canal Bridge, which was near our house and was a good vantage point to view the village. We could also see the barrage balloons over Bath and Bristol as they were caught in the searchlights, which played across the sky during the air raids. I can only remember one solitary incendiary bomb landing close to us, suspended on a nylon parachute. I tried to extinguish it with my tin hat!

CHILDHOOD MEMORIES, CIRCA 1930

by June Fry

I started school when I was three years old at St. George's. There were two teachers: Miss Fox and the head teacher, Miss Parrott, who travelled from Christian Malford by train to Melksham and then by car. There were two classrooms heated by a large open fire which was well guarded, and two playgrounds, one for the girls and one for the boys. There was no grass.

The school dentist came once a year and if treatment was needed it would cost sixpence. The school bell, which could be heard all over the village, was rung every morning and every dinner time. Most of the children went home to dinner, but those who lived some distance away, like at The Strand, would bring a packed lunch. Miss Fox cycled from Trowbridge in all winds and weather! Sunday School was held at St George's Church with two teachers, Miss Barnett and Miss Ritchens.

We used to watch the Avon Vale Hunt with the beagles from the kennels near The Knapps and the steam tractors filling with water from the brook regularly. The fish-monger would come once a week with his horse and cart, also selling fruit and vegetables. The real treat was when the Walls Ice-Cream man arrived on his tricycle. It had a large box on the front full of ices and lollies, which in those days were called Snofruites, and he would ring his bell for all to hear. There was also the Co-op van, selling bread and the butcher's van with meat. We had to fetch the milk from the farm in cans.

There was no electricity in the village. We had to use oil lamps and candles for lighting. Also there was no water in the house: just a tap outside. Even worse, there was no main sewerage, so we had to manage with a bucket in a little hut at the bottom of the garden! There was a large boiler in the kitchen, like a huge basin with a wooden lid on it and a fire underneath, which provided hot water for the weekly wash and a bath in an old galvanised tin tub. The only heating in the house was a large coal fire, with its black oven and white hearth, which were cleaned and polished every day. The oven was used to cook in most days and there was always a stew ready on the hob. Most people grew their own vegetables according to the season and never wanted for anything. Of course the chimney-sweep used to call with his black face and brushes, and we waited outside to watch for his brush appearing out of the top of the chimney, and would shout: "OK, you're through".

During the summer months we would enjoy hay-making time, riding on the wagons pulled by the lovely old horses, taking a packed lunch and plenty to drink to the fields. The children used to paddle and swim in the brook, which was perfectly clean and healthy in those days. We could even play on the road with our hoops and tops and play hop-scotch, because there was hardly any traffic about. Gipsies were quite often seen in Pound Lane with their caravans, dogs, horses and children. They caused no trouble and were grateful for water from the villagers to fill their cans.

Floods, 1935. (Courtesy Mrs J. Fry)

In the winter the road would flood down by the brook and become impassable with the water reaching from the bottom of the canal bridge right along to the old Bell Inn. Sometimes the canal would freeze over. Dozens of people would be seen skating on the top lock and even all the way to Whaddon. On a moolit night it was like magic, in another world.

FROM MRS MURIEL GOVER

Miss Elsie Gaisford was sub-postmistress for over 40 years. She was the youngest but one of a family of seven children. Her father was killed in an accident when she was four years old. Consequently life was hard for the family and they worked wherever they could. At the age of seven Elsie started working on Saturdays and during the holidays for Mr and Mrs Stockwell. Work consisted of washing floors, cleaning brass and silver, cleaning grates, running errands and delivering milk and bread. When she left school at fourteen years of age she worked every day, gradually doing more in the shop, and when Mr Stockwell died she became the postmistress. She was a staunch Methodist all her life and lived up to her principles, helping many people when they had financial or other troubles. This was evident by the large number of people who packed the church at her funeral.

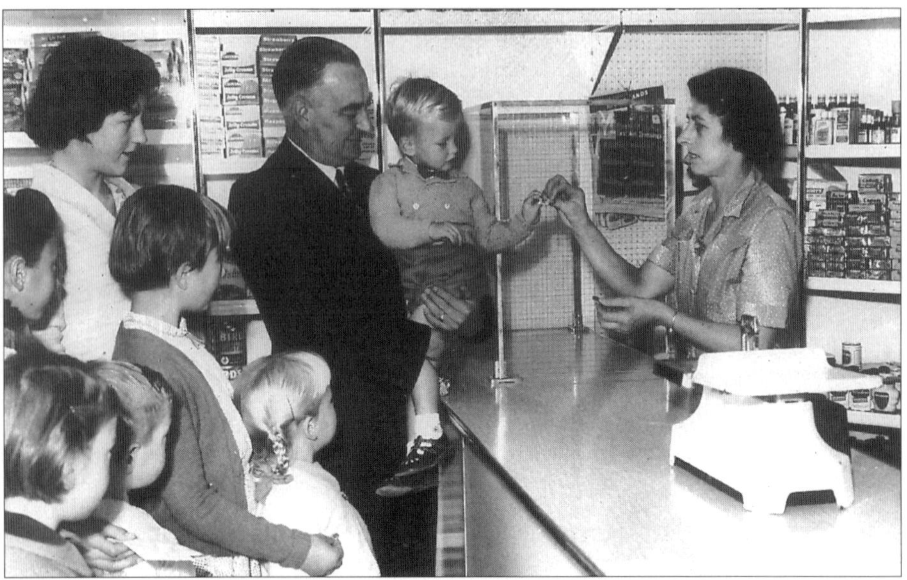

Opening of new Post Office. (Courtesy of the Wiltshire Times*)*

Semington roads were quiet in the early 1930s, although by the time the war broke out traffic was increasing. It was safe to play hopscotch, roll hoops and whip tops in the road. A large percentage of the men worked on the many farms. It was safe to wander through the fields and pick wild flowers and see plovers' nests - and be careful not to tread on them! Quite a few gypsies lived in their caravans in the lanes. The men worked on the farms, the children attended the school.

Littlemarsh was like a hamlet. Quite a few big families lived there and played together. 'Fox and Hounds' was fun in the dark, when rhubarb leaves provided good cover. The stream that flowed near Common Piece provided lovely fresh watercress: no pollution in those days.

Masters of the Avon Vale Hunt came and went, some more colourful characters than others. Sir Alfred and Lady Slade had a pet monkey. It had a room to itself with a large cage along one wall. In good weather it was on a long chain on a low roof. Its screeching and leaping about was frightening to a child delivering cream for a dinner party. Real cream in those days! The cook would be preparing the meal, invariably a pheasant, high and heaving. The grooms lived above the stables, the huntsmen in the houses. And often there were fox cubs in pens in the gardens. Every Boxing Day the beagles met at the bottom of Union Lane, as it was then known. The name changed when the Workhouse became St George's Hospital. The tramps used to gather at the bottom of the lane, waiting for the time when the Casual Ward opened and they could have shelter for the night.

Both Church and Chapel had thriving Sunday Schools. Mr Nelson Fall was superintendent of the Methodist Chapel, assisted by Miss Gaisford. The highlights of the year for a lot of the children were the Outing and the Christmas Party. At the latter there were delicious eats, including York balls, a type of soft roll, baked by Fare's Bakery at Hilperton and liberally buttered. Outings were by charabanc to Cheddar and Weston-super-Mare and later to Weymouth and Bournemouth.

Manor and Church Farms were farmed by the Jefferys Brothers and provided work for many men. Hedges, gates and stiles were always well maintained. The shepherd lived in his hut at lambing time and children were welcome to see the lambs. Haymaking time was idyllic: the lovely smell of new-mown hay and picnics and games in hay houses and armchairs. The dairymaid at Manor Farm wore a white coat over her other clothes and wellington boots, because the floor was always awash with water as she saw the milk through the cooler and into the churns. The churns stood on high stands, ready for the lorry to collect them.

Electricity arrived in the 1930s. Most people could only afford 'cottage rate' - two lights down- and one up-stairs. People cooked on a range or an oil stove. Oil stoves fluctuated with draughts and many kitchens were blackened with oily smoke and smuts.

When the circus moved from town to town the lions went through in cages, but the elephants and horses walked. Alan Cobham's Flying Display came to the village several times.

When a birth was imminent someone cycled to Steeple Ashton to summon Nurse Collier. She arrived on her bicycle, in her navy uniform, complete with black bag.

Mr Fiveash was the blacksmith, on the village green, and Mr Bishop was the wheelwright and undertaker. When there was a death he could be heard making the coffin, which was then transported on the bier to the Churchyard. Mr Stockwell was sub-postmaster and among other things also acted as a taxi, with his pony and trap. Many times the pony tired of waiting at Melksham Station and galloped home, right back to its stables.

Sugar came in sacks, vinegar in barrels, cheese large and round, complete with rind. Everything had to be weighed and measured, paraffin by the gallon, spices by the ounce, biscuits loose from tins and milk by half- and one-pint measures.

Pony and Trap. The Randall family at Littlemarsh. (Courtesy Mrs J. Fry)

Cottages stood where the Village Hall now stands. After they were demolished large hoardings took their place. There were also hoardings one side of the Canal Bridge. It was fascinating to watch the man, balanced precariously on a ladder, plastering the advertisements up with a long-handled brush. When the floods were bad, prior to 1947, cattle were washed over the wall and down to Whaddon.

FROM MR PHILIP HUMPHRIES

In January 1939 at the age of $3\frac{1}{2}$ years I was taken along to the old village school next to Semington Church to start my education. At that time we lived in Littlemarsh but by the end of the year we had moved to a house in Church Street.

My first teacher was Miss Fox, who taught the infant class. My earliest memories of school at that time are of drawing with chalk on slates, finger writing on sand trays and learning to count on an abacus. There were only two classrooms at the school. In the larger room Miss Parrott taught both the junior and older children. The school leaving age at that time was 14.

Left: Steven Humphries and dog, 1969. Right: Old School. (Both courtesy Philip Humphries)

In the winter time the two classrooms were each heated by large iron stoves, fuelled by coal and coke. On the side of the school was the cloakroom in the corner of which stood a solitary washbasin served by a cold water tap. The school toilets were fairly basic and were situated outside at the end of the school yard.. They comprised half a dozen cubicles containing wooden seats over large buckets. One of the school caretaker's duties was to empty the buckets weekly, usually on the dung heap at Church Farm. Mains sewerage did not come to Semington till many years later - in 1973.

At about the same time that I moved on into the Junior class both Miss

Fox and Miss Parrott retired. The task of educating us was taken on by the new head mistress, Miss Grace Rogers, assisted by Mrs Edna Robinson.. Lessons in the Junior class seemed to be dominated by the daily chanting, in unison, of multiplication tables, although this stood us in good stead later in life. This was before calculators and computers had been heard of. We also received lessons in English, Geography, History and other subjects. The Vicar visited once a week to give us religious instruction.

At play time the girls often played skipping games, each of which was normally accompanied by a song or chant. The boys' games were much the same as now: kicking a ball around or playing chase games.

During the war years toys were virtually non-existent so we often improvised. One of my favourites was the cotton reel tank which we made. The only traffic passing the school during my days there would normally be horse-drawn wagons and carts. .It was around 1947 before tractors started to be used on the local farms. This was when the horses started to disappear from the country scene. Many passed through Mr Ted Summers' slaughterhouse, near the canal bridge.

At playtime if we were lucky we would grab a swede or stalk of kale from a passing cart to gnaw on to keep us going till lunch time.. It was several years later before school dinners became available at Semington School.

It was a wonderful sight to see the horses pulling wagons piled high with hay or sheaves of corn on their way to Manor Farm. A steam engine pulling a threshing machine would arrive at the farm later in the year. Amongst all the noise and dust we boys would have great fun catching the mice as their nests were disturbed when the ricks of corn were threshed.. Cows would be herded past the school each morning on their way to the fields along Pound Lane where they would graze all day before returning to the farms for milking by hand. Because of labour shortages during the war years Farmer Jefferys of Manor Farm came to the school one autumn when I was aged about 9 years. He selected some of us, both boys and girls, to help him with the potato harvest. The following week we worked each day in a field near to where the Crematorium is now situated. We had to follow the horse-drawn machine as it unearthed the potatoes, picking them up and putting them in sacks. At the end of the week I received the princely wage of 10 shillings (50p). On Saturday mornings we earned sixpence ($2\frac{1}{2}$p) each for doing odd jobs at Manor Farm. This money would be spent on the weekly war-time ration of 4 ounces of sweets at one of the two village shops. Granny Hancock's shop was a wooden chalet-type building attached to the garage whilst Miss Elsie Gaisford's shop was in the house opposite the Village Hall. Milk had to be collected each day in a jug from Mr Bolwell's small dairy situated at the rear of the building in which Miss Gaisford had her shop.

During. the early years of the war evacuees arrived in Semington from London, to escape the air raids on their homes. Because our house had four bedrooms officials placed two evacuee families with us for several months. As I then had four brothers it became a little crowded at times. At school an extra class was held in the Chapel because of the influx of the evacuees.

Most of the older men in the village joined the local Home Guard and would often be seen training around the fields. Semington during the war was surrounded by an anti-tank trench, stretching from the brook just east of Manor Farm and along Church Field to the road at Knaps Hill, where large round concrete pillars were put up to help protect the village from invasion. The trench then continued , passing behind the old Union Workhouse, and finally ending near the canal.

We spent many hours fishing in the brook with worm baited bent pins, tied to sticks with cotton.. In summer the level of water in the brook would be raised by lowering the hatches at the old pump house and at the side brook, so that children and adults could enjoy the swimming.

During the dark winter evenings the wireless provided a lot of our entertainment. Outside it would be very dark: street lighting was banned because of the danger of providing targets for enemy aircraft. For the same reasons blackout curtains were put up to the windows. The village policeman would knock on your door if any chink of light was showing. A few bombs were dropped, I believe, near some farm buildings by the swing bridge, the only casualties being some fish which were stunned by the explosions and which my eldest brother brought home and kept in the bath for a while.

I can clearly remember my mother being upset one day because she had heard from the wireless that our country was at war with Germany. My elder brothers took me with them across the fields to search for the enemy. Fortunately for Adolf Hitler we were unsuccessful, or otherwise the length of the war might have been considerably shortened..

Looking back on my early years I wonder what changes today's pupils at Semington School will see in the new century.

A JOURNEY TO WORK

by Victor May

In the 1950s I used to pass through Semington on my motorbike on the way to the United Dairies at Melksham. Sadly, the Dairies have not been there for a number of years.

One frosty morning I came to grief on this road, as did many others that morning. Opposite the entrance to St George's Infirmary there used to be a row of fine elm trees, standing 60 or 70 feet high - the sort of trees that rooks would build their nests in so as to be well clear of the ground. Alas! - the trees are long gone.

Because of a heavy dew during the night the road had become wet and, as sometimes happens just before dawn, a frost. Black ice!

The road at that place runs downhill slightly and as I approached I suddenly found myself clinging to my bike and sliding down the road, flat on the ground on my side. Fortunately, I did not injure myself, as I had leg shields, but it gave me quite a fright and if anything had been coming the other way it may have been a different story.

I hear there is at last going to be a by-pass for Semington, soon to be built. This will be a blessing for the village. I only hope it doesn't mean that the shop, like so many in our villages, will close due to the lack of custom. Time will tell.

Myself with son Jonathan astride my motorbike (then fitted with a sidecar) at Weymouth in 1959. The motorcycle was a Douglas Endeavour (500cc. Twin) with a shaft drive. Not many of this model were produced.

RECOLLECTIONS

of Mrs Pam Mortimer

A year previous to the outbreak of war I started school at the age of 4 ½ years - a school that must have changed little since my father first attended there at the beginning of the Great War. A dark, dingy cloakroom with bare stone floor, one rough wooden bench, numerous pegs, and painted throughout in dark, depressing shiny brown. The "Little Room" and the "Big Room" were only fractionally better: windows were too high for "tinies" to be distracted, bare wooden floors, solid desks seating two on bench seats and a black pot-bellied stove with an enormous pipe disappearing up through a very high wooden, arched roof.

There were no pens or papers until one graduated to the "Big Room". Instead we were issued with sand trays and slate sticks. Girls and boys were kept separate, especially at playtime, with a high fence dividing the two yards. Against the south wall were the toilets - wooden seats with a hole for the buckets and an outside trough filled with sawdust.

Miss Rogers with pupils. (Courtesy Mrs P Mortimer)

When war broke out the children living in Church Street with an air-raid shelter were allocated half-a-dozen other children to race home with the moment the sirens wailed - it didn't matter that our shelter always had several inches of water slopping about over the floor, depending on the amount of rainfall. We just had to sit there until the "All Clear" sounded. Luckily they were mainly practice 'runs' and the only time that we experienced a real air raid was the night that Bath and Bristol got badly bombed. We could see the vivid sky clearly from Semington and our shelter shook from the bombs being dropped.

Back at school we chanted our tables over and over again (never to be forgotten), we read stories about "Henry Penny and the Day the Sky fell Down", we were subjected to the 'Nit Nurse' on a regular basis and every day we reluctantly swallowed cod liver oil - white from a large brown glass jar, malt extract from another large jar and one-third of a pint of milk. We carried gas masks everywhere, and this also involved "practices". The memory of the rude noises these could produce and the smell of rubber will never be forgotten.

The girls skipped and played hopscotch whilst the boys were into marbles and spinning tops - although different seasons produced different crazes - conkers in autumn, kites in spring and ice slides in winter. Lessons were strictly the three "R"s, with a weekly visit from Canon Yerburgh who gave us religious instruction.

Sunday School was a "must" and the Annual Party a highlight of the year - with Bibles, Prayer Books, etc., awarded as prizes to those who had been good all year.

The school became a private residence in 1970 and during the 1980s when the then owner had extensive alterations done to the old school yards several skeletons were discovered below the east window of the Church. There were three adults wrapped in shrouds plus a dog, and although the Police, the Coroner and a Pathologist attended the grave it was decided that as the bones were very old no further action would be taken, and the grave was covered in.

Work commences on new School, 1967.
(Courtesy Mrs P Mortimer)

EARLY IMPRESSIONS

by Edna Robinson

It was the evacuation of Dunkirk and we had just arrived in Trowbridge. There were dishevelled and wounded troops everywhere - they all looked tired and forlorn and the Park was packed with soldiers sleeping rough.

I had just arrived with my eight year old son, Michael, but we had nowhere to live. My husband, Arthur, was in the Advance Party setting up the RAF camp at Melksham. We wandered around asking everyone that we could find if they knew of any accommodation, but no one was able to help us.

We started walking in the direction of Melksham and Michael was looking more and more tired by the mile. Eventually we arrived in Semington and came across a man called George Buckley who worked for Harry Hunt, the farmer. George said that Mr Hunt owned a cottage at the Canal Bridge but that he wouldn't let it to anyone as it was reserved for the farm workers. However, I met Harry Hunt and managed to persuade him to let me have the key and we moved in. The next day, whilst we were unpacking our scanty possessions, there was a knock on the door and two workmen from the RAF camp were asking for a room. I let them stay and that same night the bombs started falling. I was glad of their support.

During the early part of the War, my daughter Jane was born. When she was old enough to go to school, I took her to Semington Village School, but they were short of a teacher, so I asked if Jane could start School if I stayed for

Village Outing, 1950. (Courtesy Mrs P Mortimer)

a few days to help until the Authorities could find another teacher. Those few days lasted for 25 years and provided me with some of my happiest memories, with Grace Burbidge and all the children that went through the School.

Later on there were English and American troops everywhere; convoys and convoys. We did not know it at the time, but they were assembling for the Invasion and Melksham Camp just kept growing. The Keevil airfield was operational for aircraft and gliders. The German aeroplanes would follow the Canal in the moonlight and from the Canal Bridge we could see the devastation at Bristol.

In spite of all the hardships and misfortunes that the War had brought, there was a wonderful atmosphere of comradeship and this was also most noticeable in the two village pubs on Saturday evenings!

Eventually we moved from the Cottage at Canal Bridge to live at Manor Farm. There were German prisoners of war staying there - they had to live in the Barn, and were not allowed into the house. At Christmas we gave them a Christmas Pudding decked with a sprig of holly; it was lovely to see the delight on their faces. They used to make slippers from leather and wooden toys for Jane. One of the prisoners hadn't heard from his family for a very long time and didn't know if his wife and children were safe. Then one day, there was a knock on the door and with tears in his eyes, he told me that he had just received a letter from his wife saying that they were all well; we both cried with relief and happiness.

Years later, when Michael was a teenager, he wanted to invite all his friends from Trowbridge High School to our house on Sundays for a Party. I used to allow this on one condition: that they all went to Church first! And that was how Mac Bennett, Mike Mortimer, Pete Shore and many more got involved with St George's Church, Semington. Having then established a group of young men in the congregation, it was the Rev. Cattarns (he of the 2 minute sermons) who manoeuvred them all into the Choir Stalls and eventually formed them into a fine male voice choir!

During his service at Melksham Camp,. Arthur was an instructor, teaching the young airmen all about instruments, and later he worked on the Gloucester Meteor, the first jet plane. After the War, we decided to stay in Semington and Arthur joined the Southern Electricity Board as an electrical engineer. We bought an old derelict pair of cottages with a large garden at Stoggy Lane - we named it "Fairacre". Arthur was Church Warden and Treasurer at the Church for many years.

Ah, Semington - what happy memories.

SEMINGTON

by L. J. Taylor

Semington has always been a special place in my life, you will gather as you read on.

The year was 1935 or thereabouts when the traffic through the village was a fraction of today's figures. There was nothing very exciting about the village - the Church, Village Hall, Post Office, two Pubs. Now it has been battered by traffic both ways and has largely lost its village identity, so much that traffic lights have been installed to enable the road to be crossed in safety, if that is possible.

Travelling from Melksham one encounters the sharp canal bridge which can surprise one if travelling too fast. On the right hand side immediately after the bridge, is the little Wharf cottage. The old wharf buildings have been removed - the cottage has been renovated and is now a delightful property. Now that the canal is increasingly active the site is even more attractive. Some years ago a footpath was constructed over the bridge for the safety of users. One wonders how the old bridge survives the massive lorries - when the bridge was constructed such traffic could not have been envisaged.

Leaving the canal bridge, there is a row of cottages on the left hand side and then we come to the Brook bridge on which has been constructed a raised pathway to cope with the flooding, which was quite frequent, until land drainage work largely remedied the problem. One now reaches the two fine houses, one on each side of the road. The one on the right is a fine old house occupied for many years by the Bruges family, who had been such benefactors to the village and church.

Continuing on the left hand side, we now come to the site of the old Bell Inn - this is no longer a pub but converted into a dwelling house. One remembers the row of beer mugs hung over the fireplace and woe betide you if you used the wrong mug. Great changes have been made at the old garage site occupied by Dick Hancock. Dick was the garage proprietor, radio engineer and general mechanic in the village, but the garage no longer exists as such and is now a car sales business.

Opposite the old garage site the Somerset Arms has been completely modernised from the original beer house into a new public house and restaurant and is immensely popular.

On the right hand side the Old Manor house still stands. This used to contain a small sweet shop where children could spend their halfpennies. The old Post Office and shop was situated on the left hand side of the road in the

Above: Canal Cottages

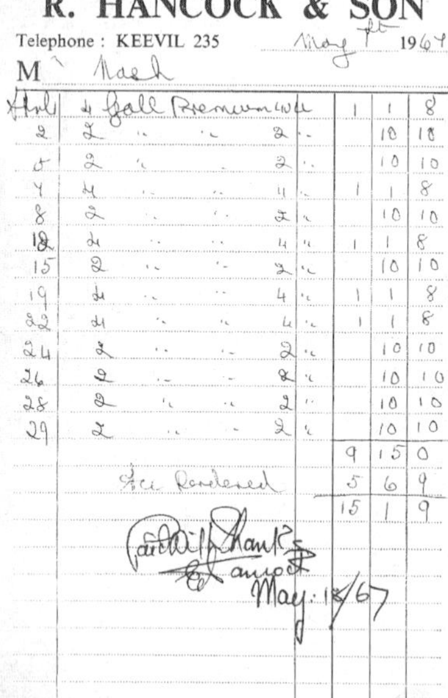

03057

SEMINGTON SERVICE STATION

Semington, Trowbridge, Wilts.

BOUGHT OF

R. HANCOCK & SON

Telephone : KEEVIL 235 May 1st 1967

Mr Nash

April	4 gall Premium @ 4/2	1	1	8
2	2 " " 2/-		10	10
5	2 " " 2/-		10	10
7	4 " " 4/-	1	1	8
8	2 " " 2/-		10	10
12	4 " " 4/-	1	1	8
15	2 " " 2/-		10	10
19	4 " " 4/-	1	1	8
22	4 " " 4/-	1	1	8
24	2 " " 2/-		10	10
26	2 " " 2/-		10	10
28	2 " " 2/-		10	10
29	2 " " 2/-		10	10
		9	15	0
	Acc Rendered	5	6	9
		15	1	9

Paid with thanks
R. Hancock
May: 18/67

Right: R. Hancock & Son Billhead.
(Courtesy Mrs J. Fry)

Below: Garage and The Bell Inn.
(Courtesy Mrs J. Fry)

red brick house (Semington brick, from its very own brickworks!) opposite the Village Hall. The Village Hall, adjacent to the village shop (which is now back on the right-hand side of the road) has proved to be a most useful asset and caters for many village activities. Behind the Somerset Arms, as far as Pound Lane, there is now a large modern housing development, including a splendid new school replacing the old one in Church Street. Returning to the left hand side, the old Blacksmith's smithy is of course no longer in existence and the properties are used for other purposes. Reaching Church Street, the Old Parsonage is still standing but used for other purposes. New dwellings now occupy practically the whole of the left-hand side towards the church. The old school is now converted into a dwelling house. Now we come to the church itself, dedicated to St. George and dating back to the fourteenth century.

Earlier on I mentioned the cottage at the Wharf. For some years this was occupied by Jack Witts, who was in fact the Verger of St. George's. He and his family kept the church in superb condition for a number of years. Few people realise the amount of work and dedication needed. The church was then lit by candles and the lighting and extinguishing of some hundred candles was no small task, together with the operation of the very large heating stove. Another task was the tolling of the church bell on funeral days, every few minutes before the service. This was done by his wife and daughter Marion.

Without wishing to ridicule the Clergy in any way, there were certain happenings which formed part and parcel of the daily routine of the church. The priest in charge of St. George's was a very elderly cleric who lived in the Parsonage. On a dark Sunday evening, a door would open from the Parsonage garden into the High Street and there would emerge the Priest robed in his black cassock and cape, carrying a lighted hurricane lantern - of course there were no street lights at the time. What a shock for the uninitiated! Another oddity which was quite amusing was that of the Cleric's sermon timing. He had placed on the pulpit a very old fashioned object shaped like a large egg timer which he religiously used to regulate the timing of his sermons, and he duly turned it up at the end.

To conclude on a personal note, I was appointed organist at St. George's in 1935, where I met and married my wife Marion, the daughter of Jack Witts, the Verger - we were married for sixty-one years. Marion lived in Semington, spending her earlier schooldays at the local school and entering into the village activities. When she died in July 1999 I thought it would be appropriate to bring her ashes to St. George's and now you will appreciate why I have a special interest in Semington.

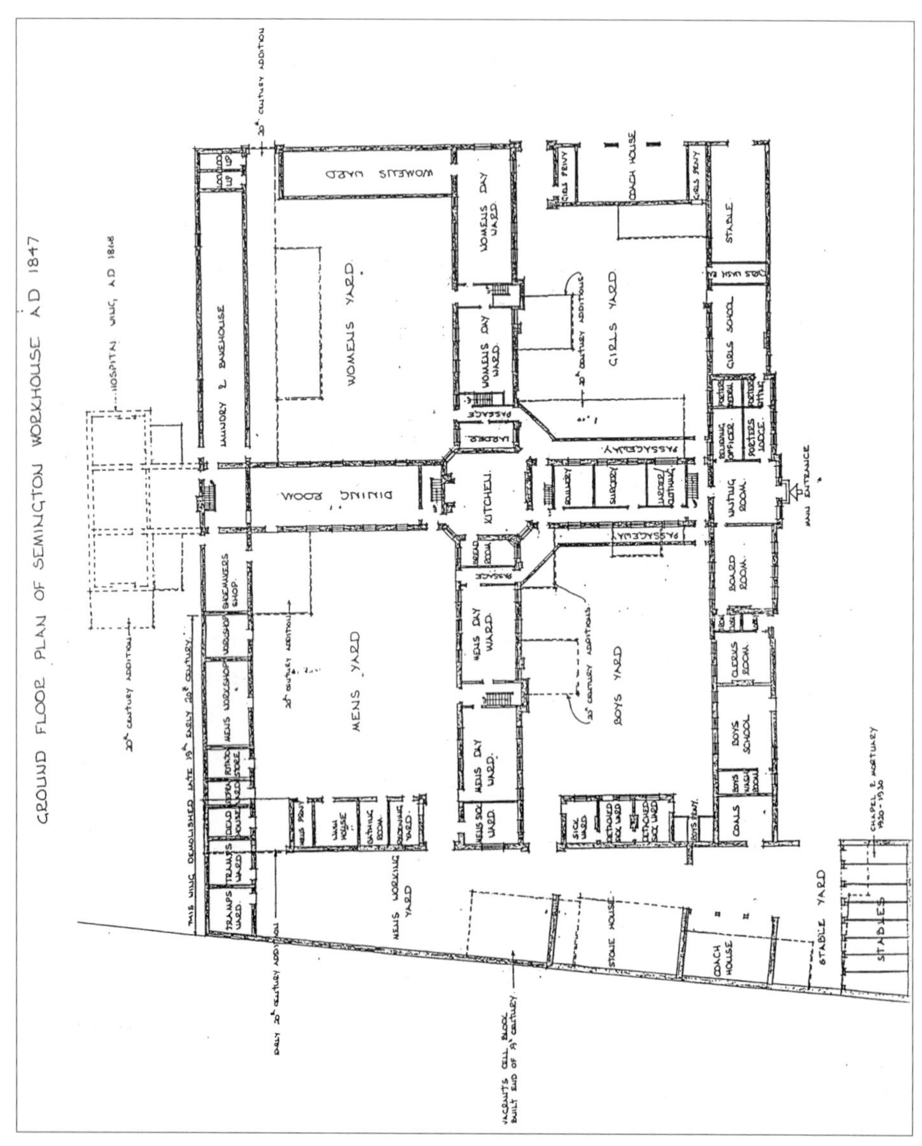

(Courtesy WRO)

Chapter 12

MELKSHAM UNION WORKHOUSE

'The evening arrived; the boys took their places. The master, in his cook's uniform, stationed himself at the copper; his pauper assistants ranged themselves behind him, the gruel was served out; and a long grace was said over the short commons. The gruel disappeared; the boys whispered to each other, and winked at Oliver; while his next neighbours nudged him. Child as he was, he was desperate with hunger, and reckless with misery. He rose from the table; and advancing to the master, basin and spoon in hand, said: somewhat alarmed at his own temerity: "Please sir, I want some more"

Charles Dickens: *Oliver Twist* (1837)

The poor are always with us and over the centuries considerable attention has been paid by those in authority to methods of helping people who, possibly through no fault of their own, have become in desperate need. There were the "deserving poor" on the one hand and those not so deserving, on the other: those who might take advantage of people of a benevolent nature. From Elizabethan times the Overseers of the Poor, legally elected but unpaid officers attached to each parish in the country, were responsible for raising rates and distributing what was necessary, either in cash or kind, to those in need.

As the population increased in the 18th and 19th centuries, however, and there were greater fluctuations in prosperity caused by bad harvests, or epidemics, the old method became unworkable. The Poor Law Amendment Act was passed in 1834. This introduced a new system, to be operated by the Poor Law Commissioners, based on the grouping together of several parishes to form a 'Union', as a means of spreading costs. From each parish, according to the size of its population, a number of people were elected to a 'Board of Guardians' responsible for raising rates and building and managing a 'Workhouse' which could accommodate all those in the whole area who were unable to fend for themselves. Therefore in 1835 the Melksham Union Board of Guardians was formed, consisting of members from Trowbridge, Melksham, Hilperton, Seend, Semington and Whaddon.

As far as Semington was concerned, as it had a small population only one guardian was elected to the Board, whereas Trowbridge had 8, Melksham had 6, Hilperton and Seend had 2 each and Whaddon had 1, making up a Board of 20 members all together. It would appear that the "NIMBY principle" ("Not in my back yard") was in force even at that time, for when the Board first met in Melksham in November 1835 it was universally agreed (with possibly one exception!) that the new Workhouse should be sited in Semington. A sub-committee was formed to decide on the exact location.

From then on the Board of Guardians met regularly at the Waggon and Horses in Semington[1] to consider plans for the new building and to raise a Poor Rate, chargeable annually to the parishes:

Trowbridge	£809.00.00
Hilperton	54.17.00
Melksham	552. 7. 0
Seend	111. 8. 6
Semington	48. 6. 6
Whaddon	2. 9. 6
	£1578. 8. 6

A Workhouse building committee was formed and advertisements were placed for plans, specifications and estimates for the proposed building. The design competition was won by a London Architect, H.E. Kendall, who based his ideas on plans produced for the Poor Law Commission. The diagram (see page 174) shows a main north-facing reception block behind which is a cruciform building dividing the ground into four separate yards, one each for men, women, boys and girls. There was strict segregation of the sexes, but two or three small detached rooms were provided in case of sickness, where a pauper might be allowed to have his wife to attend upon him. There was also a coach house, stable yard and vagrants' cells. The building, now called "St George's Court", was referred to until 1948 as Melksham Union Workhouse and was erected in 1837-38. After 1948 it was taken over by the National Health Service and as St George's Hospital was mainly concerned with geriatrics.

There was considerable opposition to the Poor Law Commission at first, because of the stark conditions in the workhouses which were being built all over the country. Not only Charles Dickens but the Editor of *The Times* and

Benjamin Disraeli joined the campaign, and there was a public outcry when in 1845 the Master of Andover Workhouse was accused of so starving the inmates that they were reduced to gnawing the bones that they were supposed to be crushing for fertilizer. A committee of enquiry was formed and in 1847 another Act was passed, sweeping away the Poor Law Commission and setting up a new Poor Law Board, which contained some provisions to make the administration of the Poor Law more humane.

Workhouse, Frontage

The problem for the Board of Guardians thereafter was how to make the conditions sufficiently harsh as to deter even the most unfortunate from wishing to become inmates, without being accused of cruelty or of actually starving the persons in their charge. The Guardians were elected by the ratepayers of the local towns and villages - people who were capable of complaining bitterly if it was felt that any undue leniency or 'feather-bedding' was being shown to the destitute poor.

The Minutes of the Board of Guardians for Melksham Workhouse provide a fascinating insight into the administration of the newly erected Workhouse. The Guardians themselves were, as mentioned earlier, pillars of the local community. Over the years the Chairmen were either local clergymen or magistrates and the members were farmers and landowners from the villages and woollen manufacturers and tradesmen from the towns of Trowbridge and Melksham.

St George's from the air. (Courtesy Mrs J. Fry)

The business of the meetings was mainly concerned with reports from the Master of the Workhouse and from the Relieving Officers (who were responsible for 'out relief'), but correspondence with the Poor Law Commission, then the Poor Law Board and, finally, the Local Government Board was invariably discussed. This correspondence shows how much control was imposed by the Government on the local community. For instance, in 1851 the District Auditor pointed out that the average weekly cost per head was seven pence a week more in the Melksham Union than in nearby Westbury. After a committee had been formed to enquire into the discrepancy it was found that the difference was accounted for by an extra allowance of one farthing for the Aged Poor, one farthing on the general dietary, one farthing on clothing and one farthing on cooking food and heating. It was decided that the Aged Poor should not be deprived of their extra allowance but that the Westbury system should be adopted for all other classes of pauper.

In 1861 a letter from the Poor Law Board reprimanded the schoolmaster for contravening the regulations by taking the boys out through the vagrants' ward instead of through the main entrance. Later a visitor (one of the Guardians) entered the schoolroom to find the schoolmaster absent and a pair of handcuffs and a chain lying on his desk. It was found that the Schoolmaster had chained a boy aged 8 to a desk for two hours. When charged with cruelty, as he had only 12 little boys in the class, he justified himself on the plea of necessity, and then resigned.

In August 1871 the Workhouse children were allowed to join the children of Semington School at their Annual School Treat.

In January 1872 another schoolmaster who was brought before the Board. for disobeying their order to postpone his projected holiday until after Christmas, declared that he was looking for another situation as the Workhouse was "a Hell upon earth". After resigning he accused the Master of drunkenness and the porter and the cook of improper behaviour The porter and the cook were dismissed but, although reprimanded, the Master stayed.

In 1880 the District Auditor disallowed a sum from the Master's accounts for the provision of beer for some of the inmates who had been asked to do dirty work. The Master protested that he had merely been following custom. The Guardians then referred to a Resolution passed by them on 17th September 1836, authorising a special allowance of beer and food for special duties. It was considered that although the Auditor's decision was lawful, in that instance the disallowance should be remitted.

In 1883 it was noted that the allowance of meat was 4 oz. for adults and $3\frac{1}{2}$ oz for children

By then it had been decided to provide a fish dinner once a week, and the tastes of the inmates were actually consulted - a far cry from 1851 and the need to conform to the dietary regime of a neighbouring Union.

There is no doubt that the Melksham Union Workhouse was a community within a community, which employed staff, paid for out of the local rates. The Workhouse also provided employment for the locality by way of requiring goods and services for both staff and inmates. In March 1881 the list of contractors consisted of four grocers, a baker, a butcher, a dairyman, three drapers, a coal merchant, a brushmaker, a wine merchant, a corn dealer, a carrier, a painter, a bellhanger, a carpenter, a market gardener and a brewer. The corn dealer, the brewer and the wine merchant were also members of the Board of Guardians. The butcher, incidentally, supplied two kinds of meat: without bone for the inmates and of a higher quality (and price!) for the officers. These supplies came not only from Melksham and Trowbridge but also from some of the local villages.

Above: The former Girls' Yard

Left: Former Women's Yard

Below: Chapel & Mortuary with vagrants' cells in the background

A study of the ages of the inmates of the Workhouse from the Census Returns[2] from 1851 to 1891 shows that there was a dramatic increase in the number of men and women aged 60 and over by 1891. There could be a number of reasons for this, one of which may have been the "Chamberlain Circular" of 1886, which authorised local municipal schemes of public works to relieve unemployment for the able-bodied. There can also be perceived a softening of attitudes, particularly towards the aged and infirm, over the years from 1838 to 1891. So by the turn of the century the Workhouse seemed to be functioning mainly as a kind of old people's home, or long-term residential hospital, which, indeed, it eventually became.

The Workhouse, which was originally isolated from the village by several fields, was in St George's Road. When the National Health Service was formed in 1948 the Workhouse was gradually transformed into a geriatric hospital and later new buildings were added. The hospital was declared surplus to Health Service requirements in 1988 and then stood empty except for one small building which appears to have been used on occasions to contain an overflow of patients from elsewhere. The new buildings were later demolished, leaving only the original structures. This building was last used as a "Day Hospital" for patients who usually lived at home but required some additional care which such a unit could provide. It also gave some respite to the carers who were normally carrying out their caring duties in the patient's home (normally a spouse or relative).

In the year 2000 work commenced to convert the main building into flats and to build a number of select houses in the grounds. The establishment is now called "St George's Court" and has become homes for those who are considerably more affluent than the original occupants.

WILTSHIRE & BATH INDEPENDENT LIVING CENTRE, SEMINGTON

In 1988 Bath District Health Authority and the Social Services Department of the Wiltshire County Council decided to improve their services to people with disabilities by establishing a Disabled Living Centre which would cover Wiltshire (except Swindon) Bath and Frome. There were 22 Disabled Living Centres in the country at this time, the majority run by registered charities. The two authorities agreed jointly to fund the project and what became the Wiltshire & Bath Independent Living Centre Trust was established. Suitable

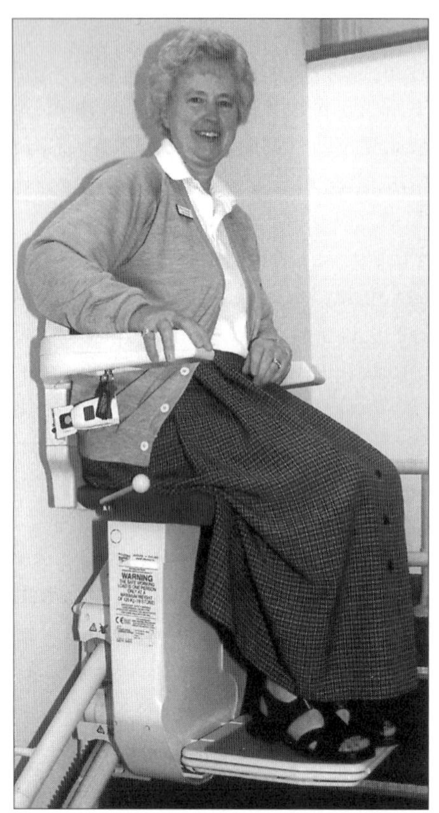

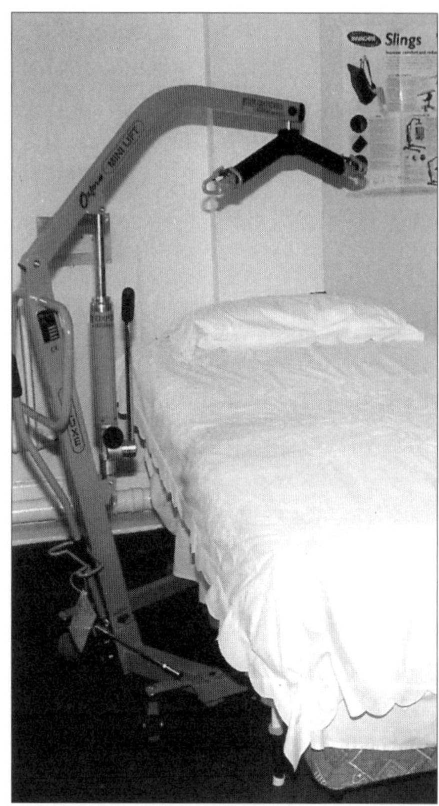

Above left: Stairlift. Right: Manual Handling Training Room
Below: Wheel Chairs

premises were hard to find but following the introduction of the Care in the Community policy in 1988 a hospital which had catered for those with mental handicap was vacated and two years later it was decided that one of the buildings on the site at St George's Semington (a village 3 miles from the county town of Trowbridge) would be appropriate and it was offered on lease to the Trust at no cost.

The purpose of the Centre is to give free and impartial advice to people who have any form of physical disability by allowing them the opportunity to try a wide range of equipment which could help them in their everyday living. This includes bathing aids, accessible baths and showers, kitchen equipment, from small gadgets to help arthritic hands, to wall cupboards and sinks which are electrically operated to adjust for height for wheelchair bound people. There is a range of mobility aids and an outdoor track for practice in manoeuvring wheelchairs. Very popular is the armchair room with power operated chairs for clients to test. All equipment is loaned free of charge by suppliers, who constantly up-date their equipment in this fast growing market. The Centre does not sell anything, but advises on outlets where items may be purchased and the recommended price. This avoids the problems which beset those who buy direct from catalogues.

Clients are referred by occupational therapists in Social Services, hospitals, GP surgeries, and many self-refer.

The Centre has a Conference Room and a Manual Handling Training Room containing beds and a range of hoists. Courses are held on Manual Handling for professional staff and home carers. Over the years the training courses have developed into an important part of the Centre's work with day courses on equipment for specific disabling diseases. A Sensory Exploration Room was funded recently by an appeal for £15,000.

The Centre is staffed by 1½ occupational therapists with administrative support. The Trust has 16 Trustees and 4 of them form the Management Committee with delegated powers for the day to day running of the Centre. All trustees are volunteers.

In August 1997 the Independent Living Centre faced a crisis. It received from the Wiltshire Health Authority a notice to quit the premises so that the whole site could be put on to the open market for sale by April 1998. With the assistance of the Chief Executive of the West Wiltshire District Council, the Wiltshire Health Authority was persuaded to give the ILC the opportunity to buy its own building at a price of £160,000 to be handed over on 1st April 1999. By a tremendous effort of fund-raising and support from the local community the sum was achieved without National Lottery help. A further £60,000 was raised for essential works and improvements to make the building more user-friendly to clients and to eradicate its former hospital image. Seven voluntary organisations associated with disability rent suites of offices adapted to their needs. They include West Wiltshire Access Group, Leonard Cheshire Disabled People's Forum, Disablement Information Advice Line, the Social Services Hearing & Vision Team, ASK, Learning Curve and Wiltshire & Swindon Users' Network. The Good Companions Community Day Centre meets weekly in the attractive Conference Room.

Contributed by Mrs Jeannette Greer,
Independent Living Centre

References

1 Minutes of the Board of Guardians for Melksham Union Workhouse (WRO H110/1-18)

2 Census Enumerators' Books for the years 1951 to 1891 (WRO)

Chapter 13

COMMUNITY GROUPS

PAROCHIAL CHURCH COUNCIL

St George's Parochial Church Council has the responsibility of co-operating with the incumbent, the Reverend David Hart, in promoting in the ecclesiastical parish the whole mission of the Church, pastoral, evangelistic, social and ecumenical. The Church is shared jointly with the Methodists, and their Minister at present is the Reverend John Rees. Until the year 2000 St George's Church was a Chapel in the parish of Steeple Ashton, although in living memory it has had its own Vestry and its own chapelwardens with independent minute book and accounts. During the year 2000 it became, with the Bishop's approval, an independent parish within the benefice. The PCC has maintenance responsibilities for the church building and churchyard. There is a standing committee, comprising the Vicar, the two Churchwardens, the Treasurer, with the Methodist Secretary and the Organist. This is the only Committee required by law. It has power to transact the business of the PCC between its meetings, subject to any directions given by the Council.

Membership of the Joint Parochial Church Council consists of 14 persons, with the Vicar as Chairman, and the Council meets generally about four times a year.

THE PARISH COUNCIL

On 4th January 1895 Semington Parish Council came into being when an Act of Parliament transferred civil affairs from the Parochial Church Council to newly formed Parish Councils.

The first Parish Council in Semington consisted of William Bruges, John Burbidge, the Reverend Stephen Chapman, William Dallimore, John Farmer, George Colledge, William Jefferys, James Noad, Henry Ridewood,

Samuel Watts, William Watts, and Ernest Wiltshire. The first Chairman was truly Independent, one Willy Bailey from Great Hinton. In the early days of Parish Councils it was possible to have a Chairman who was not a Parish Council Member, the reasoning behind this being that the Chairman could not therefore exert any influence by his voting on local decisions, as the Chairman did not have a vote and acted as an impartial referee.

In the past in many villages the Parish Council was kept in being by the dedication of one or two families who had made a tradition of service to their community. A typical example is shown in the list of chairmen and clerks which will be found at the end of the next paragraph, which shows that the mainstay of Semington Parish Council was for many years the Noad family.

By the year 2000 most villages had large increases in population, albeit with smaller family groups, so the tradition has only continued in the smaller, more isolated villages. As the population increased the number of councillors was also increased to ensure fair representation. This in turn meant that the number of options for the post of chairperson (chairman by earlier definition) was greater. In the smaller villages – as Semington once was – the parish council might have met bi-monthly or quarterly, whereas in the larger villages – as Semington has become – the Council meets monthly. The local County Councillor and local District Councillor attend meetings when possible to provide answers to earlier questions and to pass on information relating to the activities of both District and County Councils where they impinge on the village.

The following is a list of Parish Council Chairmen (or Chairpersons) and Parish Clerks from the Parish Council's inception in 1894:

CHAIRMAN		**PARISH CLERKS**	
Willy Bailey	1894-1932	Henry Stockwell	1894-1035
Joseph Noad	1932-1970	Tom Noad	1935-1987
Philip Noad	1970-1976	Angela Grodzicka	1987-2000
Ron Fry	1976-1980	Emma Jackson	2000-2002
Philip Noad	1980-1989	Roger Coleman	2002-
Doug Firmager	1989-1993		
Robert Oglesby	1993-		

Village Hall: laying of foundation stone June 1933.
Courtesy of the Wiltshire Times.

SEMINGTON VILLAGE HALL

It was a Saturday in early June, 1933, and Semington was en fete, celebrating the laying of the foundation stones of the new village hall. In the past meetings, concerts, etc., had been held in the schoolroom, which was not particularly convenient, and it was therefore decided to build a hall, open to all classes and denominations. A Committee was formed and for some years fetes and other functions had been held in order to raise the necessary £400. The Committee was delighted when the Duke of Somerset gave them a piece of land, fronting the High Street in the centre of the village, for the purpose. The Carnegie Trust donated £70 and £300 had been raised in other ways.

After a service held by the Reverend Yerburgh, Vicar of Steeple Ashton, there was a procession from the Church to the building site. Amongst the assembled residents were Mr and Mrs Bruges, Colonel and Mrs Leader and Mr Robert Grimston, the local MP. The first stone was laid by Mrs Bruges and a second by Mr Henry Stockwell, the village postmaster and Chairman of the Village Hall Committee.

The Fete, held with the object of paying off the remainder of the debt on the building, took place in a field lent by Mr Jefferys, and was opened by Mrs Grimston who was presented with a bouquet of flowers by Miss Muriel Bolwell.

Opening of Village Hall by Duchess of Somerset, October 1933.
(Courtesy Wiltshire Times*)*

When completed later that year the Village Hall was opened by the Duchess of Somerset, accompanied by Mrs Bruges, Colonel Leader and Mr Henry Stockwell.

The Council of Management which now runs the Hall is made up of eight trustees: two each from the Parish Council, the Anglican Church, the Methodist Church and the Social Club. The Trustees co-opt others to represent the children, youth, senior citizens and businesses. The Council has the assistance of a Treasurer and a Secretary and meets monthly. The business of the meetings is mainly concerned with the upkeep and finance of the building. New heating was installed and a full redecoration took place during 2000. The village Skittles teams, the Youth Club, the Kids' Klub and the Old Thyme Dance Club regularly use the hall, which is also hired out for parties, coffee mornings, jumble sales and other functions.

SEMINGTON SOCIAL CLUB

The Social Club was formed on 20th September 1960 in the Village Hall. There were two good reasons which led to the Club's foundation. First: the Village Hall had lost the £45 a year fee paid for the use of the Hall for School Dinners, as the new School in Pound Lane had its own facilities. Second: The Bell Inn was about to be closed, thus depriving the village of one of its favoured "watering-holes".

By a dint of good organisation the Social Club managed to open its Bar the day after The Bell closed in 1964. Later, in 1970, a lounge and storerooms were added to the Bar. Breweries in Trowbridge (Ushers, later Watneys) and Salisbury (Gibbs Mew) were the main suppliers together with local stores and Cash and Carry Warehouses. Nowadays Wadworths of Devizes and Moles Brewery of Bowerhill, Melksham, are the prime suppliers.

To comply with legal rules the Social Club is now a registered charity.

Under the "umbrella" of the Social Club various activities, such as skittles, Bingo, football, cricket and, hopefully soon, tennis, are played and other events are organised in the Village Hall, aided recently by a redecoration programme staffed by persons with a community service order and paid for by a lottery grant.

SEMINGTON SPORTS CLUB

Football

Local football clubs often reflect the area which they represent. Long gone are the days when it was normal for people to spend their entire lives in one village. Following the demise of large-scale employment in agriculture caused by the first signs of mechanisation, it became more usual for people to move their home to suit the availability of alternative work. Semington Rovers suffered accordingly when players left the village.

After several years of success in the 1952-56 period, winning the Trowbridge and District second division title, being promoted to the first division and becoming runners-up as well as winning two knock-out cups, the Club suffered from lack of support, often having to travel to away matches in the back of a lorry, a not unusual method of transport for football teams in those days.

The Rovers played their last game in 1956 in the Trowbridge and District League. The Club then disappeared from the football scene for 40 years, to

1999-2000 Football Team. Rear L/R: Mervyn Bray, Gary Hargreaves, Allan Clarke, Kelvin Lockwood, Michael Burbidge, Rich Bean, Phil Gregson, Ian Partington, Tony Rosling. Front L/R: Wesley Bray, Stephen Rosling, David Castle, Dan Phillips, Ben Phillips, Stuart Barber. (Source untraced).

2001-2002 Football Team. Rear L/R: Kelvin Lockwood, Wesley Bray, Michael Burbidge, Ricki King, Rich Bean, Phil Gregson. Front L/R: Dan Phillips, Steve Rosling, Stuart Barber, Allan Clarke, Tony Rosling, Nathan Walker, Stuart Donohoe. Courtesy of Kevin Lockwood.

re-emerge in 1996 with a team entered in Division Four of the Chippenham and District Sunday League.

The same winning spirit lived on and Semington Rovers secured promotion to Division Three at the end of the 1998-99 season. Success breeds success and as this book nears publication Semington Rovers have just won promotion again at the end of the 2001-02 season to Division Two of the Chippenham and District Sunday League, despite there not yet being a football pitch in Semington on which to play "home" matches - all so-called "home" games being played at Holt. Even with this handicap Semington Rovers continue to make a good name for themselves and look forward to further success and promotion in years to come.

DIVISION THREE	PLAYED	WON	DRAWN	LOST	FOR	AGAINST	GD	POINTS
SEMINGTON ROVERS	24	19	4	1	115	34	81	42
CHIPPENHAM BLACK HORSE	24	15	6	3	87	41	46	36
BIDDESTONE SOCIAL CLUB	24	15	5	4	90	37	53	35
FARMHOUSE FC	24	12	7	5	77	46	31	31
CHRISTIAN MALFORD	24	11	5	8	86	59	27	27
SIR AUDLEY'S ARMS	24	9	6	9	72	73	-1	24
AFC UNICORN	24	10	4	10	56	59	-3	24
SOUTHWICK SPORTS & SOCIAL	24	7	7	10	54	53	1	21
ROWDE	24	8	5	11	62	75	-13	21
CORSHAM PARK RANGERS	24	6	7	11	58	88	-30	19
HARE & HOUNDS	24	8	2	14	44	73	-29	18
NORTH STAR B	24	4	5	15	45	73	-28	13
PLOUGH	24	0	1	23	31	166	-135	1
					877	877		

2001-2002 League Table (courtesy of Chippenham Sunday League)

Cricket

As with football, all of the village cricket fixtures have to be played "away" because as yet Semington does not have its own facilities.

Youth Club

There is currently a Youth Club meeting one evening a week in the Village Hall. The present lack of outside recreational facilities restricts the possible activities, but with the soon to be opened hard tennis court, off St George's Road, there will be another sport available. If proposed developments in the village go ahead as planned then further sports will be possible, both in an enlarged community hall and on the adjacent recreation field.

Skittles

Skittles is played regularly by the four Semington teams (2 ladies' and 2 men's). All teams play in the local league and enjoy good support.

THE EVERGREEN CLUB

The records of the Evergreen Club go back to 1961 when the leader was a Mrs Nash, who appears to have continued in that office until 1993, when Mrs Daisy Jane took over. The Club meets every other Tuesday afternoon at the Village Hall from 2.30 to 4 p.m. There are at present 19 members.

This is a Club for the older-aged group of the village, who enjoy a game of cards. They play Whist and occasionally have a game of Bingo. They are self-funded and raffles are organised to provide funds for them to have lunches together in the Village Hall, so that the members can enjoy the more social side of the Club.

Mrs Betty Bonham took over from Mrs Daisy Jane four years ago, as Chairperson and Treasurer. To enable the Club to obtain insurance cover she had to join the WRVS, as had the previous leaders. This also entails providing the WRVS with financial records on an annual basis.

SEMINGTON OLD THYME DANCE CLUB

The Club opened on 4th October 1993 with 12 members, having been started by Mrs Pat Burrows, the then Organiser of Semington Good Companions Community Day Centre, in order that the Good Companions could learn to dance and benefit from the exercise. It was funded for the first six months by Wiltshire Rural Initiative, and meets in the Village Hall on Mondays from 2.15 to 4.15 p.m.

Now it is a separate entity with a membership of just under 50. It has become not just a place to learn old time sequence dancing for people of all ages under the able instruction of Peggy and Eric Whatley, who are to be congratulated on their patience and good humour, but a venue to meet with friends and chat. Members come from far and wide: from Melksham, Holt, Trowbridge, Broughton Gifford and Seend, apart from Semington itself.

Other activities include American Teas, with contributions from members, a 'Close Down' Tea in June, usually supplied by the Club and produced by the Committee, after which there is a break until September; and a Buffet Luncheon before the Christmas closedown.

SEMINGTON GOOD COMPANIONS COMMUNITY DAY CENTRE

This is a group for the over 60s which meets weekly. These meetings were originally held in what used to be the 'Red Cross' House (now the 'Old Rectory') then in the Village Hall, but later moved to the Conference Room at the Independent Living Centre.

The members meet at mid-morning and either chat or play various games, then have lunch followed by a talk or some entertainment, or have another games session. From time to time outside coach trips are organised to visit different attractions, such as Moreton-in-Marsh (for the market), Warwick Castle, Hereford, Poole and other places within a range of travelling times of not more than one and a half hours so as not to be too tiring.

SEMINGTON WOMEN'S INSTITUTE

The present Semington W.I. was officially formed in January 1997. However, there was a thriving W.I. here in the village in the 1930s., which continued until the early 1960s. At this time A Young Wives Group was formed and many of the younger members transferred to this, leaving an insufficient number to continue as a W.I.

W. I. 12th Birthday Party, January 1946. (Courtesy Mrs P. Mortimer)

Thirty or more years later it was decided by a few ladies that it could be time for another try and to date this "try" has become a successful W.I. The new Group now has 23 members and we meet once a month in St George's School. Our activities are wide, varied and very entertaining - no home-made jams for this W.I.!

Most of the Speakers and Demonstrators illustrate their talks with slides and artefacts and subjects range from a talk by a member of Hampton Court School of Embroidery to a Kikuyu Wedding. Country-house style Denman College, situated in Oxfordshire, offers a wide range of courses to all W.I. members throughout the year. We also socialise with other local W.I.s, especially West Ashton, when we join in each other's celebrations and rambles.

Summed up, perhaps, by the following:

Scones, jam, apple pie
Original W.I.
Achievement, travel, high-fly
Ambitious W.I.
Don't deny – try
Join the W.I.

BIBLE STUDY GROUP

Various Bible study and prayer groups have existed in Semington over the years. Some just met in Semington, whilst others met in Semington, Steeple Ashton and Keevil, by rotation.

Semington's current Bible Study Group continues on from the Group that rotated around the villages, but also includes people who wanted to meet to study God's Word, following the Alpha Courses held in Semington from 1997.

The Group meets twice a month in people's homes. Usually up to twelve people are present - anyone is welcome to attend. The evening starts with singing and prayer and then one of the group will lead the study, which can be challenging, is always interesting and very often a lot of fun.

THE PHOENIX GROUP

The Phoenix Group rose from the ashes, as it were (hence the name), of a National Women's Register group that had been running in Semington since September 1989. In September 1994 the members decided to form their own completely independent group instead - and the Phoenix Group began.

The Group, which currently has fourteen members, meets every month. The members are all women, but their men are included for activities such as skittles evenings or theatre visits. Most meetings take place in members' homes. It is a social group, enjoying a range of activities, including the ever-popular annual Safari Supper.

THE VILLAGE FETE

Village Fêtes are similar to football teams in that they run for some years and then lapse for a while.

Many years ago Semington used to have a large annual flower and vegetable show, when many villagers worked on the land and it was almost second nature to them as well as a financial necessity to grow as much produce as they could. Some even took on allotments in addition to their gardens. With people now having to travel to work they have less time available for gardening and the tendency is to opt for a plot of land which requires minimum upkeep consistent with looking nice. The move now is to have a produce stall at the Fete along with other stalls such as bric-a-brac,. books, Granny's Attic, Tombola, bowling for a prize, coconut shy, toys, and a plentiful supply of ice cream, cakes, tea, coffee and soft drinks.

Semington's Fête has traditionally been held in the garden of Brook House and is normally organised by a small group of about six people, with many more helping on the day.

THE FRIENDS OF St. GEORGE'S PRIMARY SCHOOL

The long established Friends of St George's Primary School, popularly known as 'The Friends', get together once every half term to plan and suggest ideas for fundraising and social events. These meetings are informal and friendly and open to anyone who is a parent or relative of children at the school or a member of staff. Help is always welcome in whatever form by donating items, attending or helping out at events.

Past events have included Millennium Family Disco, Children's Bingo, Jumble Sales (which provide an excellent opportunity for turnouts) and the annual end of term BBQ. Last year's was wet and wild, but enjoyed by all.

The money raised from these events is thankfully received and provide for the children extra educational/recreational resources as well as 'Fun' trips out like the pantomime at Bath Theatre Royal and the awaited visit to the Arc Theatre at the end of Summer term to see 'The Secret Garden'.

The children enjoy the Pudsey Bear biscuits in November, when we support 'Children in Need'.

The Friends have an AGM in September, when a committee is elected.

TODDLER PRAISE

Toddler Praise is a monthly service in the Church, particularly for mums and children, but anyone is welcome. There can be between 2 and 20 people present each month.

It began in 1991 at the suggestion of the Mum & Toddler Bible Study group. We want the children to discover that God is special and make Church a place where they look forward to being.

It is very informal - we praise God together, using simple 'action' songs and prayers. The children enjoy playing small percussion instruments, we have a short story and often there are things for the children to take home. We end with squash, coffee, biscuits and a chat.

THE KIDS' KLUB

Kids' Klub began in the autumn of 1991 and is for 7-11 year olds. There had been a similar club in the village a few years previous to this.

We meet fortnightly in term time, either in the Village Hall or on the school field. We have 20 members at present and each evening we have a variety of activities which can include a Bible story, drama, games, craftwork, singing and prayer.

We have an annual 'Prizegiving' service, which for the past three years has been followed by a barbecue and swimming at Brook House.

The aim of the group is to share the love of Jesus with the children and, of course, have fun!

THE 31 CLUB

This began in 1992 as a natural progression from the Kids' Klub. 12-15 youngsters aged 11-15 meet monthly - half of these evenings are in a home where we play games, watch videos and look at various issues from a Biblical perspective. We also go swimming, ten pin bowling and to Queensway Chapel in Melksham for games evenings. During the summer we have played tennis and been swimming at Brook House, with the kind permission of Michael and Tara Bruges.

The main aim of the group is to have fun and share the love of Jesus with these youngsters, helping them to grow to have a personal relationship with him.

THE "SOUP RUN"

The Trowbridge and District Churches Soup Run is now into its sixth year, and for the past two years the co-ordination has been in the care of Keith and Rosemary Earley from Semington. The Thursday evenings are covered by five local teams - three from Steeple Ashton and two from Semington and North Bradley. The sixth local team has been going out on one Saturday evening per month since one of the Trowbridge churches had to drop out. There are fifteen churches involved, each team being manned by three people and there are many more behind the scenes involved in sandwich preparation and making soup and cakes. Many disadvantaged people come to the Soup Run for help, some regularly and others during very difficult times in their lives.

St George's C of E Primary School always kindly donates unsold items of clothing at the end of their fund-raising sales and have been very generous at Christmas time.

CHAPTER 14

THE FUTURE

For nearly two hundred years the dry-stone construction hump-backed bridge over the Kennet and Avon Canal withstood all that traffic could inflict on it. The bridge, which had been built to carry a maximum weight of 8 tons was adequate for farm carts, brewery drays and horse-drawn stage coaches. Latterly it has had to withstand a daily traffic flow of 2,000 forty-ton lorries plus 18,000 other vehicles. To enable the bridge to survive even this far it was necessary in 1998 to fit a concrete 'cap' weighing 160 tons as a holding measure.

The new diversion is to the east and goes under the canal. This involves the construction of an aqueduct and because the re-opened canal cannot legally be closed, in turn this gave the need for a side 'cut' to be excavated to take the canal around the aqueduct site while building goes ahead and allows the canal to remain in use for the increasing number of boaters.

The Wilts and Berks Canal is currently the focus for canal restoration. Several lengths in the Chippenham and Wootton Bassett areas are already in water. More lengths are being cleared of trees, infill material and rubbish by volunteer working parties.

It will not be possible to follow exactly the entire original route because, for example, much of Melksham has been built over parts of the canal and although it is still possible to see short sections and the occasional bridge, large scale reconstruction in this area will not occur. Current thinking is to seek a new route, rejoining the Kennet and Avon Canal at some other point.

Semington's housing stock is increasing while this book is in preparation. The old Melksham Union Workhouse was used as a hospital until 1988 and then closed. The main building is now being converted into residential units with a housing estate being added in the grounds. From this development the village will gain a hard tennis court.

Further proposals for more housing are currently being discussed by a developer with West Wiltshire District Council, who are the local housing planning authority. If this scheme comes to fruition then the enlargement of the village will continue and Semington will gain a new village hall and a long sought-after recreation field.

Crystal ball gazing will not provide definitive answers to questions. However, a look at Government legislation, which requires Wiltshire to build many tens of thousands of extra homes in this decade, certainly indicates that considerable change will take place in the county. Determining what this increase in the housing stock may produce in terms of employment needs, transport requirements and the subsequent enlargement of the distribution network, can only lead to the conclusion that pressure on all essential services will grow.

BIBLIOGRAPHY

Primary Sources:

Census Enumerators' Books for the years 1841 to 1901.

Chapelwardens' Accounts, Semington, Wiltshire Record Office 714/18.

Minutes of the Board of Guardians for Melksham Union Workhouse, 1845-1891 WRO Catalogue No. H11 110/9-18.

Bruges Family Papers WRO 3238.

The Duke of Somerset's Papers WRO 1332/16 and 1332/17.

The Parish Registers & Bishops Transcripts of Semington: Baptisms and Burials to 1837 Wiltshire Family History Society, 1989/92.

The Domesday Book: Wiltshire, Edited by Caroline & Frank Thorn, from a draft translation prepared by Caroline Thorn, Chichester, Phillimore, 1979.

Inquisitions Post-Mortem, Returned into the Court of Chancery in the Reigns of Henry VIII, Edward I & Edward II, British Record Society, Ltd., 1908

The Victoria History of the Counties of England: Wiltshire, Vols. VII and VIII.

The Victoria History of the Counties of England: Hampshire, Vol. II.

Secondary Sources:

Allsop, Niall, *The Kennet & Avon Canal*, Bath, Millstream Books, 1987.

Aubrey, John, *Topological Collections*, collected and enlarged by John Edward Jackson Wiltshire Archaeological & Natural History Society, Devizes, 1862.

Bates, Allan, *Directory of Stagecoach Services*, Newton Abbot, David & Charles, 1836, Reprint 1969.

Bray, S.M. , *The Devizes Branch*, Picton Publishing, 1985.

Bryan, T., *The Great Western at War 1939-1945*, Hawes Publishing, 1995.

Chandler, John, *John Leland's Itinerary, Travels in Tudor England*, Gloucester, Alan Sutton, 1993.

Chandler, John (Ed.) *Printed Maps of Wiltshire, 1787-1844*, Trowbridge, Wiltshire Record Society, Volume 52, 1998.

Chandler, John, 'Stagecoach Operation through Wiltshire' Historical Monograph for South Wiltshire Industrial Archaeological Society, September 1980.

Cobbett, William, *Rural Rides*, with Introduction by George Woodcock Harmondsworth, Penguin English Library, 1830 Reprinted 1967.

Crowley, D.A. (Ed.) *A Wiltshire Tax List of 1332*, Wiltshire Record Society Vol. XLV, 1989.

Cullingford, Cecil N., *A History of Poole*, Chichester, Phillimore, 1988.

Dalby, L.J., *The Wilts & Berks Canal,* Lingfield, The Oakwood Press, 1971.

Davis, Thomas, *A General View of the Agriculture of Wiltshire,* The Board of Agriculture and Internal Improvement, 1811.

Defoe, Daniel, *A Tour Through the Whole Island of Great Britain, 1724-6.* Reprinted with Introduction and Notes by Pat Rogers, Penguin English Library, 1979.

Dickens, Charles, *Oliver Twist,* London, Everyman's Library, 1838-41, Reprint 1963.

Dodge, Alan, *Freshford, The History of a Somerset Village,* 2000, Freshford Publications, 2000.

Geddes, Isobel, *Hidden Depths: Wiltshire's Geology and Landscapes,* Bradford on Avon Ex Libris Press, 2000.

Gillam, Beatrice (Ed.), *The Wiltshire Flora,* Pisces Publications, 1993.

Gover, J.E.B., Mawer, Allen, & Stenton, F.M., *The Place Names of Wiltshire,* Cambridge University Press, 1939.

Harper, Charles G., *Stagecoach & Mail in the Days of Yore,* Vols. I & II, London, Chapman & Hall, 1903.

Holcroft, H., *An Outline of Great Western Locomotive Practice, 1837-1947,* Locomotive Publishing Co. Ltd. (undated)

Holcroft, H., *The Armstrongs of the Great Western,* London, Railway World Ltd., 1953.

Holt Magazine: *Last Look at Holt Junction for Devizes Branch, 1967.* Holt Magazine Editorial Board.

Leigh, Chris, *Western Steam in Colour,* Branch Lines, Ian Allan Publishing Ltd., 1992.

Lenten, H. T., & Colledge, J. J., *Warships of World War II,* London, Ian Allan

Liveing, the Rev. Henry G.D., MA. *The Records of Romsey Abbey, An Account of the Benedictine House of Nuns (AD 907-1558),* Winchester, Warren & Son, c.1910.

Mann, J. de L., *The Cloth Industry in the West of England from 1640 to 1880,* Gloucester, Alan Sutton, 1987.

Morley, Geoffrey, *Smuggling in Hampshire & Dorset,* Newbury, Berks Countryside Books, 1983, reprinted 2002,

Norris, Beale & Lavis, *Railmotors, Edwardian Enterprises,* Wild Swan Publications, 1987.

Pevsner, Nikolaus, Revised by Bridget Cherry, *Wiltshire,* in The Buildings of England series. second edition, Penguin Books, 1975.

Phillips, Daphne, *The Great Road to Bath,* Newbury, Berks, Countryside Books, 1982.

Ponting, Kenneth G., *The Woollen Industry of South-West England,* Bath, Adams & Dart, 1971.

Priddle, R. & Hyde, D., *GWR to Devizes,* Bath, Millstream Books, 1996.

Ramsay, G.D., (Ed.) *Two Taxation Lists 1545 & 1576,* Devizes, Wiltshire Archaeological & Natural History Society, Vol. X, 1954.

Robertson, K., *Odd Corners of the GWR from the Days of Steam,* Gloucester, Sutton Publishing

Ltd., 1999.

Rogers, Kenneth, *Wiltshire & Somerset Woollen Mills*, Edington, Pasold Research Fund, 1976.

Rogers, Kenneth, *Steeple Ashton, Village History & Guide*, Lacock Print, Committee of the Friends of Steeple Ashton, 1986.

Small, Doug (compiler), *The Wilts & Berks Canal*, Stroud, Tempus, 1999,

Smith, Betty, *Steeple Ashton, Our Wiltshire Village*, Gloucester, Alan Sutton, 1989,

Tanner, G.H.J., *The Calne Branch*, Oxford Publications, 1972.

Tate, W.E., *The Parish Chest*, 3rd Edition, 1969, Phillimore & Co., Chichester, reprinted 1983 by permission of Cambridge University Press.

Taylor, S. *Semington Jubilee Book*, Semington, 2002.

Thomas, Edward, *In Pursuit of Spring*, London, Thomas Nelson & Sons, 1914.

Wroughton, John, *An Unhappy Civil War, Experiences of Ordinary People in Gloucestershire, Somerset & Wiltshire, 1642-1646*, Bath, The Lansdown Press, 1999.

INDEX

Abattoir, 127, 133,
Abingdon, 138, 140
Adair, W., 35
Aircraft crash, 13
Allum, J., 22
All Souls College, Oxford, 31, 65, 66, 109
Andrews & Drury, 60, 62, 88, 92
Anglican & Methodist co-operation, 34
Anglo-Saxons, 11
Aqueducts, 12, 95, 98, 138
Arnulf de Hesdine, 127
Ashton Manor, 25
Avonmouth, 137
Avon, river, 127, 139, 142, 145, 151
Avon Rubber Company, 131
Avon Vale, HMS, 13, 124, 125
Avon Vale Hunt, 124, 154, 158, 160
Awdry, A., 29, 127

Bacchus, RFA, 81
Bailey, Miss, 38
Bailey, S., 47, 151
Baker (Bennett), Betty, 39
Barn, 96
Barnett, Miss, 158
Bartletts Farm, 68
Bath, 89, 90, 91, 137, 139, 157, 167, 181
Beach, Anne, 32, 33
Beavan family, 29, 37
Beauchamp, Bishop R., 25
Bell Inn, 45, 86, 87, 88, 100, 159, 171, 172, 189
Bendy family, 33, 62
Bennett family, 23, 40, 157, 170
Berryfield, 80,
Bible Study Group, 194
Bigwood, R., 65
Bird family, 74
Bishop, Mr, 38, 161
Biss, river, 14, 152
Blacksmith, 42, 173
Boatbuilding, 127, 134
Bolwell, Billy, 151, 165
Bolwell, Miss M., 187
Bonham, Mrs B., 192
Borthwick, A., 68
Boundary Commissioners, 17
Bournemouth, 161
Bowyer, Miss, 38
Bradford-on-Avon, 16, 80
Bradley, 14, 16, 25
Bratton, 14, 127
Brickfield Farm, 45, 115
Brickyard, 45, 131, 132, 173
Briden, 106
Bridge House, 100
Bright, Glenys, 112
Bristol, 90, 137, 139, 140, 152, 157, 167, 170
Bromham & Rowde, 149
Brook Cottage, 96, 100
Brook House, 97, 102, 195-7
Broughton Gifford, 16
Brouncker family, 15
Brown, W. R., 20
Bruges family, 19, 28, 29, 31, 32, 62, 65, 66, 73, 74, 88, 109, 171, 187, 188, 197
Buckland, 105
Buckley, G., 169
Burbidge, Mrs, 82, 170
Burrows, Mrs P., 192
Butler, R. W., 35
Butt, C., 132
Butterflies, 119, 121
By-pass, 13

Calne, 139
Camerton, 140
Canal Cottages, 100, 133, 171, 172
Canal Terrace, No. 552, 106
Canham, R., 68, 69
Carnegie Trust, 187
Cattarns, Rev., H. R., 40, 170
Chalfield, 15, 16
Chamberlain, Rev. G., 65
Chapelwarden, 26, 29, 30, 33, 34, 71
Chapel, Wesleyan, 34, 35, 37, 38, 39, 80, 151, 157, 161, 165
Chapman, J., 65
Charles I, King, 12
Cheddar, 161
Chippenham, 90, 139, 140, 141
Chippenham Sunday League, 190, 191
Christian Malford, 158
Choir, 40
Church Farmhouse, 12, 15, 45, 47, 96, 105, 106, 107, 115, 117, 118, 155, 161, 163
Church Street, 46, 52, 163, 167, 173
Church Street, Nos. 26 & 27, 12, 16, 96,

108, 109
Civil Defence, 157
Civil War, 12, 15, 109
Clarke, D., 143, 146, 148
Coach House, 12, 96, 98
Coaching, 89, 90, 91
Coal, 140, 141
Cobbett, William, 9
Cobham, A., 161
Collier, Nurse, 161
Collins family, 132
Collins, Georgina, 23
Compton, Bishop H., 37, 43
Cornish Riviera Express, 146, 147
Cottle, Miss, 19
Courts Baron, 87, 88
Covered Dry Dock, 136
Cox, 105
Crawley, Rev. H., 32
Crematorium, 164
Cresswell Down Farm, 14
Cricket, 191
Crop marks, 66
Cuff, Mrs., 80
Curtis, M., 66

Dallimore family, 19, 32
Dark Ages, 11
Davis, T., 113, 114
Defoe, Daniel, 9
Devizes, 16, 57, 88, 90, 91, 92, 138, 142, 145, 149, 154
Dickens, Charles, 175, 176
Domesday Book, 9, 11, 17, 127
Dowes, M., 75
Down, C., 45
Dragonflies, 123
Drinkwater, J., 71
Duck Race, 20, 21
Dyer, R., 47

Earley family, 197
Edgar, King, 11, 25
Edgeborough Building Co., 106
Edington, 14
Edward VII, King, 76
Edwards, C., 142
Electricity, 161
Elizabeth I, Queen, 43
Elizabeth II, Queen, 13, 20
Evergreen Club, 192

Fall, N., 161
Farleigh Castle, 57
Farr family, 35, 38
Fawley, 155
Fête, 46, 76, 83, 187, 195
Fish, 123
Fisher, H.B., 35
Fisherton Jail, 128
Fitzmichael, 15
Fiveash, Mr., 151, 161
Flora & Fauna, 119
Flooding, 142, 159
Flower, F.B., 35
Font, 29
Football, 189
Forsyth, W.H., 35
Foxhangers, 145
Fox, Miss, 158, 163, 164
Friends of St George's School, 83, 195, 196
Frome, 141, 181
Frome United Breweries, 87
Fry, June, 45

Gaisford, Elsie, 159, 161, 164, 165
Gaisford, G., 74
Gaisford, Rev. T., 65
Gale, H., 31
Garratt, J & J., 132
George V, King, 12, 76
Ghey, J., 65
Gibbs Mew, 189
Gilbert, Mrs S., 22, 82-85
Glass, W., 106, 118
G.L.N., 151-55
Gloucester, 128
Goddard, 127
Godfrey, Mrs., 80
Good Companions, 184, 192, 193
Goods label, 143
Gore, T., 17
Gover, Mrs M., 159
Granary, 95, 106, 107, 118
Great Hinton, 25
Great Western Railway, 137, 140, 142
Greenwood, 62, 63
Greer, Mrs J., 184
Grimston, R., MP, & Mrs 187
Guley, M., 74
Gulliver family, 31, 35, 47, 62. 65, 74, 88, 154

Hancock family, 36, 75, 152, 164, 171. 172

Hart, Rev. David, 185
Harvey, "Drainer", 152
Hawkins, R., 62, 65
Hayward, J., 65
Heal, Alison., 22
Heald, W., 62, 65
Heath, J., 132
Heath. Ralph, 127, 128
Helliker, Thomas, 12, 128, 129
Henry VIII, King, 9, 43
Hervin, Mrs., 80
Hibbed, J. J., 37
Highfield Close, 51
Highfield House, 97, 103, 118
High Street, 42, 55, 173
High Street, Nos. 11 & 12, 100
High Street, Nos. 69 & 70, 97, 103
High Street, No. 71, 100, 104
Hill, M., 33
Hilperton, 14, 17, 88, 115, 161, 176
Hippersley, 127
Holt, 16, 45, 92, 142, 145, 147-9, 191
Holton, 106
Home Guard, 152, 165
Honniball, A., 74
Howell, A., 132
Hulbert, 106
Humphries family, 79, 163
Hungerford, 142
Hunt Close, 124, 125
Hunt, H., 169
Huntmaster's house, 124
Hutchings, B., 74
Hyde, D., 143

Independent Living Centre, 181-4, 193

Jackson, E., 23
Jane, Mrs D., 192
Jansson, 57, 58
Jarvis, Maurice, 29, 30, 134
Jeffreys Brothers, 47, 106, 107, 117, 118, 155, 161, 164, 187
Joint Parochial Church Council, 35, 39, 185
Jolly Butcher, The, 45, 87
Jones, J., 128
Jubilee Celebrations, 18, 21, 84

Keeble family, 22
Keevil, 14, 32, 34, 92, 127, 170
Kemp, W.L., 35
Kendall, H.E., 176
Kennet & Avon Canal, 12, 13, 44, 57, 62, 106, 128, 133, 137-42, 145, 152, 199
K & A and W & B Junction, 139, 141
Kids Klub, 188, 196
Kitson family, 17, 108, 109
Knapps, The, 50,158
Knubley, Canon, 32. 34
Korean War, 35

Langley, E., 74
Large family, 134, 135
Lavington, 147, 151
Lea, 57, 58
Leader, Col., 188
Ledyard, J., 134
Leland, 9
Lewis, M., 75
Linzey, J., 37
Listed Buildings, 95
Littlemarsh, 43, 44, 47, 53, 68, 88, 115, 160, 162, 163
Littleton, 31, 43, 44, 47, 68, 69, 71, 73, 88
Littleton Green Farmhouse, 12, 68, 96, 99, 115
Littleton Mill, 12, 15, 70, 71, 97, 110, 126-28, 131, 137, 152
Littleton Mill Farmhouse, 12, 68, 100, 104, 110
Littleton Mill House, 97, 104
Littleton Wood Farmhouse, 12, 43, 68, 96, 99, 115
Lloyd, Sylvie, 119
Lock, Commander W., 81,
Lock House, 12, 136, 137
Locks, 136, 137
Lockwood, Kevin, 22, 190
Locomotives, 147, 149
Lomas, Miss, 38
London, 89, 90, 91, 139, 140, 142, 145, 152, 157, 165
Long family, 15, 17, 18, 31, 39, 65, 66, 76, 127, 152
Louise, Princess, 20
Loule, J., 65
Lowis, E., 29

Mammals, 119-21
Manor Close, 52
Manor Farmhouse, 12, 15, 45, 47, 79, 95, 106, 107, 115-18, 155, 161, 164, 165, 170
Manor House, 12, 45, 97, 102, 152, 171
Marks, D., 71

Marsh, J., 28
Marston, 19
Mary, Queen, 76
Masters family, 22
Matravers, W., 62, 66
Mauritius, 81, 82
May, J., 65
May, Victor, 166
McBryde, Dr. Hugh, 106, 118
Melksham, 15, 17, 18, 20, 76, 79, 88, 90-92, 132, 133, 138, 139, 141, 142, 162, 166, 169-71, 176, 199
Melksham (Bowerhill) RAF, 80, 147, 169, 170
Melksham Park Farm, 115
Mercer, A., 66
Merebrook, 14
Messiter, W., 87
Methodists, 37, 38, 188
Methodist Church Council, 35, 38
Meuton, H., 74
Miles, Job, 87
Miles, Ruth, 74
Millard, H., 62
Miller, T., 66
Mills, 11, 127
Milsom, T., 65
Moles Brewery, 189
Moore, F. L., 35
Moore, Rev. A. R., 34, 81, 82
Mortimer family, 167, 170
Mudhoo, Canon, 81
Munday, A., 75

Naish. family 127, 128, 133
Nash, Mrs., 80, 192
Newbury, 149
Newhouse Farm, 115
Newtown Farm, 115, 137
Noad family, 38, 128, 129, 130, 186
Noad & Son, 126
Norman, 106

Odstock, 28
Old Railway Farmhouse, 95
Old Thyme Dance Club, 188, 192
Orchard, The, 53
Ordnance Survey, 17, 61, 62, 66, 67
Osborne, J., 74
Osmon, F., 75
Outmarsh Farmhouse, 12, 66, 94, 95, 115, 118
Oxford, 17

Palmer Grove, 54
Pans Lane Halt, 149
Parish Council, 12, 34, 185, 188
Parliamentary Forces, 15, 16
Parochial Church Council, 34, 35, 39, 185
Parrot, Miss, 158, 163, 164
Parsonage, 32, 45, 73, 173
Passion, A., 127
Passions Mill, 71
Patience Mill, 43
Patney & Chirton, 145, 149
Paxcroft, 43, 44, 73
Paxcroft Brook, 152
Paxcroft Farm, 45, 47, 115
Pearce, Mrs., 80
Penny Platt, 43, 45, 47, 131
Perrett family, 35, 132
Petrol pumps, 153
Pewsham, 139
Phillips, J., 87
Phoenix Group, 195
Pillbox, 137, 150, 152
Pitt family, 15
Pocock family, 62, 65, 66, 107, 116
Pony & trap, 162
Poor Law Act, 12, 175
Post Office, 45, 49, 131, 160, 171
Pound Close, 51
Pound Lane, 55, 159, 164, 173
Priddle, R., 143
Priestley, J., 138
Pulpit, 27
Pumphouse, 70, 152, 153, 165

Rabbitts, F., 47, 75
Radstock, 141
Ragged Smock, 43, 87, 88, 90, 154
Randall family, 162
Read, J., 128
Reading, 137, 152
Red Cross House (Old Parsonage), 96, 101, 173
Rees, E., 75
Rees, Rev. John, 185
Refuse Collection, 12
Reptiles & Amphibians, 119, 121
Rifle range, 70, 152
Ritchens family, 33, 39, 158
Rivers, Baron, 15
Robinson, Mrs. E., 39, 164, 169

Rogers, Miss G., 164, 167
Roman occupation, 11
Romsey, Abbess of, 14, 15, 25, 127
Rood Ashton, 17
Rosling, T., 22
Roundway Down, 12, 15, 16
Royalist, 16

Sainsbury, J., 33, 73
Salisbury, 90, 114,
Salisbury, Bishop of, 31
Sawtell, J., 144, 148
Saxton, 56, 57
School, new, 13, 20, 21, 73, 81, 84, 85, 165, 168, 173, 189
School, old, 12, 72-75, 77, 78, 80, 151, 163, 164, 167, 169, 173, 179
Scott-White, Sally, 119
Seend, 90, 142, 145, 149, 151, 176
Seend Head Mill, 131
Semington Brook, 15, 68, 127, 151, 152
Semington Chapel Trustees, 65, 73
Semington Church, 11, 20, 24-26, 33-35, 38, 44, 96, 151, 158, 161, 168, 170, 171, 173, 188
Semington Halt, 12, 13, 66, 142, 143, 145, 147-9, 154,
Semington House, 12, 45, 97, 101
Severn, river, 139
Severnside, 155
Seymour, Lord Thomas, 17, 25
Shemp (Scamp), J., 28
Shop, 48, 49, 131
Shore, P., 170
Sims family, 65, 66
Skittles, 188, 191
Slade, Sir A., & Lady, 160
Slocombe, Mrs P., 68
Smart, J., 65
Smith, G., P/C, 47
Social Club, 20, 188, 189
Somerset, 15
Somerset Arms, 21, 45, 86-89, 97, 152, 171, 173
Somerset Coal Canal,. 138, 140, 141
Somerset, Duke & Duchess, 15, 25, 31, 38, 39, 62, 65, 66, 73, 87, 88, 106, 107, 116, 117, 155, 187 188
Somerset Way, 51
Somner, Thomas, 71, 127
Soup Run, 197
Southwick, 14, 16, 25
Speed limit, 13
Sports Club, 189
Springform, E., 45
St. George's Court, 55, 176, 180, 181
Staverton, 128
"Steam", Swindon, 144, 146, 148
Steeple Ashton, 9, 14, 16, 25, 26, 28, 34, 37, 39, 71, 127, 161
Steeple Ashton Church, 11, 25, 26, 31, 32, 39, 44, 76, 88
Stocker, E., 75
Stockwell family, 18-20, 38, 159-61, 187, 188
Stoggy Lane, 170
Stokes, W., 87
Stone tablet, 27
Strangers Corner, 43, 44, 47, 115
Street lights, 12
Summers, T., 164
Swaine, G. H., 35
Swindon, 114, 139, 140

Tannery, 127. 133. 134
Tarrant, W., 16
Taylor, A. R., 74
Taylor family, 23,
Taylor, G., 66
Taylor, L.J., 171
Thames, river, 139, 140
Theobalds, J., 134, 135
Thingley, 45
Thirty-one Club, 197
Thomas, Edward., 9
Thompson & Noad, 117
Thomson, A., 28
Tilley, 106
Timbrell, T., 28
Timsbury, 141
Tinhead, 15
Tithe Map, 1837, 62, 64, 65, 73, 88, 109
Titt, C.H., 35
Toddlers Praise, 196
Tollhouse, 92, 133, 139-42
Tombs, 29, 96, 98, 154
Tramper, 151
Triangulation Stations, 62
Trowbridge, 14, 16-18, 20, 57, 76, 88-92, 128, 138, 145, 152, 158, 169, 170, 176, 179
Truefull, Charlie, 151
Tucker, P., 44
Tunnicliff, 57, 59
Turnpike Act, 92
Turnpike Commissioners, 65

Twyford, J., 17, 109
Tyburn Ticket, 26, 28, 31

Usher James, 20
Ushers Brewery, 189

Vagg, H., 45
Vaudry, Rev., 71
Vestry, 33, 34, 71
Victoria, Queen, 12, 18, 20, 76
Village Hall, 12, 22, 38, 88, 151, 162, 165, 171, 173, 187-9
Village Outing, 169
Vincent, T., 62
Vooght, P., 8

Wadworths Brewery, 147, 189
Waget, Thomas, 25
Waggon & Horses, 88, 176
Wainhouse, William, 32
Waller, Rev. J., 37
Warminster, 90
Water & marsh birds, 119, 122
Watson, Miss, 157
Watts family, 19, 35, 37, 47, 65, 153
Weeks, J., 66
West Ashton, 14, 16, 25
Westbury, 45, 91, 141, 145, 149, 178
Westminster, 138
Weston family, 22, 23
Weston-super-Mare, 161
Weymouth, 161
Whaddon, 9, 17, 18, 68, 115, 127, 145, 151, 159, 162, 176
Whaddon Church, 11, 17, 18, 97
Whaddon Grove Farm, 17, 115
Wharf Cottage, 94, 95, 138, 171, 173
Whatley family, 192
Wheeler family 33, 35
White, W., 65, 66, 106, 118
Whitworth Brothers, 57, 59
Whorwellsdown, 14, 16, 17
William the Conqueror, 11
Wilshire family, 37, 65, 73
Wilts & Berks Canal 12, 44, 57, 62. 106, 133, 137, 138. 140-2, 199
Wilts and Somerset Railway, 141
Wiltshire family, 37, 66
Wiltshire Wildlife Trust, 119
Wilts Rifle Volunteers, 152
Wiscombe family, 79, 80
Witts family, 173
Womens Institute, 21, 22, 193, 194
Woodward family, 22
Woolmington, Muriel, 22
Workhouse, 12, 44, 49, 88, 97, 161, 165, 166, 174-78, 180, 182, 199
World War I, 12, 35, 44, 76, 151
World War II, 13, 35, 54, 83, 124, 137, 147, 152, 155, 157, 164, 167, 170

Yerburgh, Canon, 78, 157, 168, 187
Yorkshire, 128
Youngman, Canon, 78
Youth Club, 188, 191